God Consciousness
The journey of a science driven psychic medium

By
Isabelle Chauffeton Saavedra

Copyright © 2013 Isabelle Chauffeton Saavedra
All rights reserved.
ISBN-10: 061593501X
ISBN-13: 978-0-615-93501-0

DEDICATION

To A and M my beautiful children,
our Consciousness is what makes us for ever inseparable

CONTENTS

Foreword - vi
Acknowledgements – xii
Preface - xv
1 Can you hear me? Yes I can! The case of Dustin Dodd – 1
2 A quest and a search prompted from beyond the grave - The case of Virginia - 22
3 Welcome to Earth - 40
4 Learning to be me - 43
5 My first brush with death - 49
6 Connecting with energy for the first time consciously - 56
7 Mind over matter? The case of Psychokinesis - 65
8 Déjà vu? - 77
9 "Papé" (Grandpa) on the streets of Istanbul - 81
10 Full body apparition - 89
11 The awakening - 92
12 Connecting with Consciousness: A child's aptitude we should encourage - 99
13 On my way to a career path - 111
14 Visiting another life - 116
15 "You can only see if you pay attention"–NOT! - 124
16 Past life regression, reincarnation, or is it really in the past? - 130
17 Of movement, time and entanglement - 136
18 Getting more attuned, getting "entangled" – Meditation - 140
19 Is Meditation the only way to attain an altered state of consciousness? - 147
20 Going back to this "other life" - 153
21 What do we learn from our parallel lives? - 160

22 Getting in touch with the After Life and Consciousness research community - 168
23 Meeting with Gary Reece, NDE experiencer - 172
24 Meeting Dr. Melvin Morse and Learning CRV (Controlled Remote Viewing) - 190
25 Bill Guggenheim - 208
26 Mastering my own reading technique The importance of tangible validations in readings - 211
27 Searching for missing people - 222
28 Finding an engagement ring in the laundry room! - 226
29 Describing a house to a T while trying to retrieve information about a robbery - 228
30 The importance of cross validations in mediumship – the Glorying, a spirit rescue - 234
31 Deathbed visions - 241
32 Demystifying the whole ghost hunting business - we need to find new terminology for Consciousness and the whole area of research on Consciousness - 248
33 (God) Consciousness is the answer we all have been waiting for - 253
About the Author - 255

FOREWORD

"In this universe, where all beings and every created thing are interdependent and united, like the links of an endless chain, there is space neither for the supernatural, nor for the miraculous. Laws, as rigid and inflexible as those which govern matter, rule the invisible world. To understand the admirable mechanism of this law, there is but one way, the patient study of them." Spiritist Philosopher Leon Dennis (1846-1947)

SCIENTIFIC MEDIUMSHIP

In this book, which profoundly touched my soul and spirit, Isabelle Chauffeton Saavedra describes herself as a science driven psychic medium. She teaches us that we are stardust, but the stars bear our Consciousness. In doing so, she is reflecting the current cutting edge of science that describes the Universe as first and foremost consisting of information.

This information in turn shapes the natural laws of the Universe, which in turn determine the physical properties of matter. There is as much space between the various atoms and molecules of our physical bodies as is found between the stars in the Milky Way. This new "information science" describes reality as ultimately being a timeless spaceless all information domain. Children, who have died and returned from this reality that transcends our physical bodies, simply call it "God".

For most of us, "scientific mediumship" is an oxymoron, such as "jumbo shrimp" or "military intelligence". The two words simply do not seem to fit together, from either side of the science versus paranormal debate.

Mediums bristle at the idea that their intuitive and psychic skills could ever be questioned with the tools of science. Scientists bristle at the idea that there might be forces and laws in the Universe that cannot be measured or analyzed in the laboratory.

I was such a scientist; a medical scientist skilled at resuscitating critically ill children, at the University of Washington. My faith in the strict materialistic philosophy of science was shaken when many of those children we rescued from certain death, spoke of a love and an intelligence that exists beyond the physical body. One girl told me "I was never so alive, as the time I was dead". Another girl spoke of her near death experience by saying: "I wasn't dead, I wasn't dead at all, I was alive, some part of me, my spirit, was still alive, even though I was dead".

My faith in science as an investigative tool of all aspects of reality, including the phenomenon of medium ship, was reinforced when I worked with Isabelle analyzing her remote viewing skills. Isabelle was courageous and confident enough to put her psychic abilities on the line by allowing me to test her psychical abilities. I would identify a physical target that currently exists such as an iceberg in the Artic. I would not in any way identify the target to Isabelle.

I was shocked and astonished when again and again she could accurately with considerable description describe such targets. Even more fascinating were the times when she almost described the target, but missed in some ways.

For example, she described the large ice mass under the aforementioned iceberg as being a large submarine, very cold, and hollow. In fact, this iceberg had a large submersed hollow core to it.

Isabelle embraced these mistaken perceptions. She saw them as opportunities to refine her skills, to be more complete and accurate.

An iceberg hidden from her ordinary perceptions is simply a cluster of information. It has a distinctive size, temperature, shape, history, and cultural context. All of these bits of information combined create what we then label as a particular "iceberg" in the Artic Ocean.

This distinctive informational signal is embedded in the greater informational timeless spaceless domain. The informational domain is a scientific term, others call it "the higher consciousness" or simply an immanent god within nature. If Isabelle can recognize the unique energy signal of the cluster of information we understand as "iceberg", she can also recognize and access other unique energy signals.

Each of us has a unique energy signal, a consciousness that we call our spirit, or our soul. Our memories, our body shape, our hopes and dreams and desires, our personal history; all combine to create the energy signal that is uniquely ours. Those we love who have died also have a distinctive energy signal, which still exists; albeit in a way that we cannot precisely define. Perhaps it cannot be measured in a laboratory, yet anyone who has suffered the loss of a loved one has at one point or another felt such an energetic contact. It might come in the form of a vivid dream, a caress of the face, spoken words such as "Mommy, I'm okay, don't cry for me", or even the blooming of a plant out of season. It is largely forgotten that the first great birth of spiritualism in Western culture came about with the blessings of science. Early scientists associated with the spiritualist movement of the late 1800s included William Crookes, William James, Alfred Russell Wallace, Charles Richet, and Pierre Currie among many others.

William Crookes was a renowned chemist and physicist who discovered the element thallium. His theories of "radiant matter" led directly to modern theories of electricity. William James was a physician and psychologist, known as the Father of Modern Psychology. Alfred Russell Wallace was a co-discoverer of Darwin's theory of evolution.

Charles Richet was a physician and Nobel Prize winner for his theories on allergy. He went on to describe in detail "the sixth sense", a "cognition that senses vibrations not accessible to the ordinary senses". His book The Sixth Sense was the first scientific description of this natural psychic ability. Pierre Currie received the Nobel Prize in physics for his and his wife Madame Currie's work on radioactivity. He was one of the early scientists who studied mediums with a true skepticism. True skepticism of course involves both scientific rigor and a willingness to accept the results of scientific inquiry, no matter what those results might show.

Mediumship then fell into its own dark age, throughout the 20th century. Materialistic based science flourished, with exciting advances in computer technology, engineering, airplanes, automobiles, and all the many aspects of material reality that we currently enjoy. Mediumship floundered in wave after wave of fraudulence mediums and con artists being exposed by skeptical scientists. Medical science with heart transplants and antibiotics to cure diseases seemed poised to defeat death itself. In turn, the interest and desire to understand the human spirit that might exist beyond death, waned.

Remarkably, it is medical science itself that led to a resurgence of interest in a soul or spirit that might survive death. In the past thirty years, Critical Care physicians such as myself had the technology to resuscitate critically ill patients who seemed to be clinically dead.

When revived, they spoke of a reality beyond this one. They came back from death with a greater understanding of the purpose of life. Virtually all of the children I resuscitated from near death stated that the purpose of this life is to learn lessons of love.

One of the best documented adult near death experiences was the experience of Robert Kennedy, a San Francisco physician. He said of his experience of being engulfed by unconditional love at the time of death: "if my experience is any indication of the meaning of life, it is to learn to love like that, no maybe more to the point, to learn to be loved like that".

Isabelle Chauffeton Saavedra is but one of a host of modern scientifically driven mediums. They see themselves as spiritual scientists, learning to explore the unseen spiritual reality that we all co-exist within. Just as there are theoretical physicists, and experimental physicists, this new breed of mediums have both the theoretical side and the experimental side.

The experimental scientific mediums are taking psychic mediumship to a new level. They are working with comatose patients to serve as an informational bridge between them and their loved ones. They are becoming trained as grief counselors to bring psychological rigor to their work with bereaved clients. They are learning how to effectively work with law enforcement to help in solving crimes involving missing persons.

Examples of the current cutting edge of theoretical scientific mediumship investigations include Gary Schwartz MD PhD and his graduate student Julie Beischel Phd. Gary Schwartz is a scientist at the University of Arizona who has extensively studied mediumship. Julie Beischel has her doctorate in pharmacology and toxicology before founding the Windbridge Institute.

Her institute has a battery of tests that are administered to mediums with a resulting certification process if their psychical abilities can be documented.

x

The great Brazilian Spiritist and Medium Chico Xavier (1910-2002) said that mediums must keep current with advances in science. If they do not incorporate the new scientific understandings into their art and practice, they run the danger of becoming mere con artists and charlatans, Chico Xavier wrote this in the 1940s.

Chico Xavier regularly subjected his own medium ship to scientific scrutiny, and worked closed with Brazilian intellectuals including physicians, scientists and engineers, in perfecting his craft. He is one of the most studied mediums of all time, with an accuracy rate of over 70% in terms of his predictions and messages from departed loved ones. He wrote over 400 books detailing his precise and accurate psychic readings. He did not charge clients and lived a simple life consistent with his ideals.

We now enter into a new era of the reunion of spirit and science.

Isabelle Chauffeton Saavedra is one of a new breed of science driven psychic mediums. She has taken up the challenge of Chico Xavier. She has advanced her craft to a higher level by using the tools of science. I am grateful that she has paused from her important work and research to write this book. We have much to learn from it; it is an inspiration as to what true medium ship can achieve in the modern era.

Melvin L Morse MD

Dr. Morse has studied near death experiences in children for over 20 years, as a Critical Care Physician affiliated with the University of Washington. He wrote Closer to the Light, Transformed by the Light, and Where God Lives: Paranormal Science and How Our Brains are Connected to the Universe.

ACKNOWLEDGMENTS

This book would have never seen the light (pun intended) without many people and wonderful souls I would like to thank.

First I would like to thank you, my sister, Helene Chauffeton for being so persistent with our parents in requesting a "little brother". Without you, I would not be here today! You have also guided me through the roughest time of my life, I'll be eternally grateful for that.

I want to thank my wonderful parents Renée and Jean Chauffeton for loving me, guiding me and supporting me in every endeavor I took without questioning. Your unconditional love has been my guiding light.

Many thanks go to my close knit family in France, my cousins Jean-Pierre and Monique, Magali and Christophe for their help in producing the song that goes with this book, my cousin Caroll, my uncle Jean (†) and my aunt Jeanine for their unconditional love.

This book would not exist without the incredible support of my husband and love of my life Cesar Saavedra. You kept providing for our family while I was spending hours writing and still helped me with the children after work and much more. I love you till the end of time.

I wrote my book mostly when our children were in school, but sometimes, when an idea came up, it could not wait for the next day and I spent time writing taking time away from you A and M. So I want to thank you for your patience with your mommy. It was quite an adventure.

A special thank you to you my friend Nicolas Bigosinski for always challenging my mind with your healthy skeptical attitude.

A very special thank you to you Dr. Joe. O'Connell for your support in the community of After Life researchers. Your enthusiasm and compassion are a force to be reckoned with.

I want to thank all my Facebook friends and fans of my page for their incredible support and demonstration of love and light. You all inspired me to write this book.

I want to thank the Helm and Aberton family (Steve, Robin and Shelly) for their support and for letting me share their stories in this book. You are part of my journey.

My gratitude and admiration go to Dr Erica Goldblatt Hyatt, Assistant Professor and Department Chair of Psychology at a religious college in Pennsylvania, for bringing new, edgy yet serious concepts into her curriculum for her students. It will be my second year in 2014 lecturing for your class and it is an honor.

I want to extend a huge personal thank you to Dr Melvin Morse, for believing in me and guiding me through the process of writing a book. Your friendship means a lot to me.

And last but not least, none of this would have been possible without the wonderful souls in their pure energy state who have shared with me their private lives through the ethereal veil of their souls, helping their families and friends understand that their consciousness is still very much alive and present, intrinsically part of our Universe(s); with a special place in my heart for Dustin and his wife Aim.

PREFACE

The grief of losing someone we love is a necessary step in our understanding of the deep connection we have with our loved ones. But it is a very hard, intense, sometimes too hard to bear journey that one has to take on.

Although there is no way around that journey, there are ways to ease the load of the pain we carry on our shoulders and in our heart.

Some may turn to religions, others to different activities or support groups. All of these are good ways to go through our grief.

I am not a grief counselor nor am I a doctor, but a psychic medium.

And as such, I have encountered my share of bereaved parents, sons, daughters, cousins, friends and have witnessed first hand how the knowledge of being connected to a crossed over loved one can help tremendously on that difficult journey back to some sort of normalcy.

As beings of energy residing in a body *having the experience*, we have the privilege to see, hear, smell, touch, taste and feel… Those are our six senses…

We think our senses are only to the number of five… This is such a limitation.

The first barrier that we need to drop and the first preconceived idea that we need to forget is that we can only use these senses in our bodily form.

The combination of all our senses is what makes us who we are.
Yet, <u>our body does not see, touch or feel; our Consciousness does.</u>

We can still experience these senses while in a dream state… How can we touch someone when we are not even awake?
We have all experienced that, haven't we? Touching or being touched, or hugged in a dream can be as powerful as touching or being touched while being awake, even more.

How can people with disabilities still see or hear? They learn to use their mind's ears and eyes.

They use their other senses to compensate.

How does a person who has been vision impaired all her life know what purple is? They can "feel" the color vibration or the color's temperature and associate the colors with emotions.

We are in a society that only gives credit to the first five senses. We are hardly coming out of the Stone Age in regards to our sixth sense: There are now more and more awareness of the fact that we can "feel" things and that the information we "feel" can be trusted.

This is the sixth sense. Though there are still a lot of resistance and skepticism, it is at least no longer a taboo to talk about it and it's even become a huge part of research around the world in many different forms.

What is interesting is that we are in fact coming back to basics. We are now learning to trust our senses again when it was something we knew instinctively to do before society taught us to rationalize everything.

Why do we have to learn back what we knew before? How did we forget? It is very simple: because material evolution has gradually made our brain and DNA forget that we are pure energy, we are all KNOWING. That capability is what I call the seventh sense.

Like an entangled particle in a quantum system at our deepest level, we KNOW instantly what's going on with the rest of the system. We are so PART of our Universe(s), so PART of its energy web that we KNOW.

If we learn how to conquer again our sixth sense, that same sixth sense which generations after generations our ancestors have been told to ignore, we will undoubtedly be whole again as beings of energy.

We will all KNOW and feel the connection we so much need to feel with our departed loved ones.

Forget light speed. Knowing is instantaneous.

Like the incursion I made into a "past" life while sitting on a plane in 1995. I knew instantly who I was and what was going on. It took me years to understand I had connected with another possibility of me, in a quantum fashion; but I knew when it happened that who ever I was seeing was me and what ever was happening was more real than reality.

We are ALL KNOWING, not only a handful of chosen ones.

We ALL have the ability to connect to the energy around us, because we are ALL made of the same elements; the very same elements that were here at the beginning of the Universe(s) and that are still making the Universe(s) as we know it in our space/time frame of reference.

We share the same particles and the same waves of energy. We are matter and we are waves. We morph as the Universe(s) morphs.

Our body is just a good TV or Radio receptor. TVs and radios don't KNOW how to do things; they just function the way they were built for. They just process information, they process the signal they receive and turn it into sound energy and images.

Our body does not know much. Does our brain know it's a brain? I don't think so.
Does our heart know it's a heart? Not either. They have just been programmed to execute a function. Like a TV, a radio or a computer.

But our Consciousness KNOWS.

Our Consciousness knows our body can have chills and feel emotions when in the presence of emotional energy.

*"We are conscious despite of our brain"

*"The brain reduces our ability to know everything, it reduces the level of knowing of Consciousness and gives a false idea of time and space which quantum physics is starting to explain."

(*Eben Alexander III, MD – Author of "Proof of Heaven", a journey into an amazing NDE (Near Death Experience))

Classic medical science will tell us that our Consciousness is a byproduct of brain activity.

Brain activity clearly induces production of <u>Awareness</u> or not if lack thereof. But I firmly believe that <u>Consciousness</u> is NOT the byproduct of brain activity and is only processed by our brain, like an external signal.

In this book I will show that <u>we can train our brain to open more and let in the flow of Consciousness that connects us all in ONE.</u>

From the moment I was born to my current adult life, I have come to understand the intricate relationship between Consciousness and the Universe(s), two inseparable entangled concepts.

This book is about my journey and each stepping stone that has triggered a new understanding of that relationship. I will go through all the concepts I propose as potential hypotheses for what we commonly call the "After Life".

I hope my own journey can help those who are seeking answers.

We are stardust, but the stars bear our Consciousness.

CHAPTER 1

Can you hear me? Yes I can!
The case of Dustin Dodd

The Facebook messaging sound caught me by surprise. It was "a friend of a friend". Her name is Robin.

I had never connected with Robin; she was family to two people I had given a reading to previously. But I did not know her, and had actually never been on her personal page.
She bluntly asked me a question that would profoundly change my life:

"Have you ever connected with someone who is in a comatose state due to trauma, injury or surgery?"

"No! No I have never done it before!"

I am a psychic medium.

But until then, I had been doing readings for people who wanted to connect with their deceased loved ones.

This was a first.

Yet the more I was thinking about it, the more it became obvious that there would be no difference! It is about connecting with Consciousness whether it is attached or filtered by a body or not. The connection I establish is with the energy of Consciousness not with any person's brain.

So whether the person is alive and well, deceased, or alive but not responsive, the end result is always the same, I connect with Consciousness not with a body.

That's when I met Dustin.

Robin proceeded to tell me she had a friend in a coma, without giving any other information, and that she was sure the family would love to receive signs from him that he is ok.

I told her that as long as the family gave me their consent to do the reading I would be honored to try and connect with Dustin.

Once the legal technicalities were out of the way, I told her I would do the reading but I did not know when, as I usually proceed with all my other sitters.

All my readings are done at a distance, in a double blind setting. My sitters do not know when I do the reading and I don't know anything about the sitters and the person they wish to communicate with.
I don't see them, I have no idea who they are and where they are on the map.
It takes away all the possibilities of doubt from the sitters that I could be fishing information in their facial

expressions or do what's called a cold reading.

A few days passed and on the night of November 5th 2012, I felt a strong urge to sit down at my computer and start receiving from Dustin.

I meditated and started to write. *retreating*
Once I was done, I felt his energy retrieving and I sent the email to Robin to relay to Aim, Dustin's wife.

They both wrote back to me validating and commenting on what had come through.

Their comments sent a shock wave in my soul.

As I was reading them, coming from two different people in two separate emails, cross validating the information that had come through, I realized something extremely unique and important had just happened.

Dustin, loving husband and father of six beautiful children, locked in a deep coma, incapable of communicating verbally or physically, had been heard.

Not only did he have tangible validations to share with me to reassure his family that the connection was real, he also came up with a list of things he needed to help him improve his state of awareness!

As the family implemented what he had asked for during our connection, Dustin showed signs of cognitive improvement.

Below is the exact email transcript of my reading, with Dustin's wife (Aim) and Robin's commentaries in *italic*. Their comments are embedded in my text as they did send them to me that way.

Please keep in mind that <u>my readings are not done in a literary manner, but are written as the perceptions, images and sounds come to my mind</u>, hence the very raw writing.

"Good evening Aim, — *Conversational, engaging*
Thank you for trusting me attempting connecting with your loved one.
Aim (Aim): Hi there! I have been trying to find time to write you, and give you feedback on my husband's reading. First off, I wanted to say thank you so much! I had chills reading the whole thing. Ok, so I copied and pasted the email, and just thought it would be easier for me to give you feedback by breaking it down.

I decided to try and make the connection tonight. For most of the time during the reading I was given by your husband his own viewpoint from bed, which never happened to me before. I also talked like "I" being him, which also never happened to me before. But sometimes "I" was him and sometimes "I" was me.

My readings are unedited. I write down what I feel, see and hear. But for the sake of comprehension I will make annotations when "I" is me and when "I" is him.

The following is the unedited reading:

"As I write this, I hear the word "cat" by the way so I have to write it down
Robin: Favorite animal
Aim: Ok so we had the kitten, and an unfortunate accident happened, and we lost him in the wash machine. I was so upset, and cried for days, literally all day long. My husband said that if he dies first, he will let me know the kitty is ok, and he would tell him sorry for me.

(Me talking) I see a clear plastic bottle like a coke bottle but clear, there is water in it.
Aim: On the little table in front of his bed, I had left a big smart water bottle there.

Seems that there is a window on his left.
Aim: Yep, there definitely was a nice big window to his left.

I don't see the windows but I see light coming from his left
I am aware there is a door to my right. There are two doors to my right actually.
But one goes outside my room.
Robin: His name is Dustin. When I read the reading, I knew Valerie (Dustin's sister) was at the hospital with him. I texted her and asked if she was awake, as I knew my next questions would be out of left field and she would think I was kinda crazy. She replied she was at the hospital. I texted back: "How is Dustin doing, assuming you are with him?" She replied yes, she was just leaving. I then said: "Totally random question but is there a window or light source to Dustin's left?" She said yes... Then I said: "Are there two doors to his right?" She responded: "You are freaking me out!!" I told her to call me. She did.

During our conversation I confirmed that there was a window to his left, two doors to his right and that only one opened.

On the right next to the foot of the bed there is something either on a chair or a chair. I don't know if it is the back of the chair or something else but it looks like a hollow shape like a toilet seat up. I don't know what that is.
Robin: The end of his bed has a curve to it, which she felt resembled an open toilet lid.
Aim: He had a bottom piece that they put on the bottom of his bed, and from his viewpoint, would look exactly as you described.

(Him talking) My bed is narrow and there is nothing in front of me, I am facing a wall.

I am aware I am lying on this bed. I can see the bottom of the bed.
I need music!
I miss music!
What bothers me is the silence!
It's silent; it's too silent!
Robin: The music, he loves music. She (Dustin's sister) had asked him the night you did the reading. It was another thing that shocked her. I told her to get him some music please. And her response was shear disbelief for a moment. She said: "How did you know?" I was like: "How did I know what?"
- *She said, "that I asked him if he wanted music!!"*
Valerie said she asked Dustin if he wanted some music and he squeezed her hand. They are now playing music for him and/or leaving the TV on for him.

Aim: This man loves music like no other. Music literally is his life, and he has it constantly playing. I bought a little boom box for his room, and it's on all the time now.

There is this one doctor with dark hair, tall, thin. He's the one checking on me, but I can sense a second person, I can't see well, it's a lady, she's blond.

Aim: I cant quite tell if she is a nurse or a doctor That night, he had a tall nurse, with dark brown hair, he was very tall and thin, and the nurse that took over his shift was a blond lady. Both very nice, and Dustin liked them, I could tell.

You came to visit me with a white top that had some brown or darker color on the sleeves with a round neckline.
Robin: Valerie says Aimee is always wearing a brownish colored cardigan.
You sat to my left. I can't see on my sides, please stay in front of me.
He is again showing me this young blond lady with a ponytail.
Robin: His wife Aimee is a blond who wears her hair in a ponytail all the time. She sits to his left while she is with him.

I know something's wrong with my right side
Aim: It turned out he had a lung infection on his right side. It was making him so very sick.

Doctors concerned with my liver or my right upper quadrant
Robin: He had a brain tumor that was removed, and his brain was shifting to the right, they put in a shunt to stop it. He developed a blood clot in his lung

I am bored.
I need animation.
I need stuff on the walls; these walls are boring.
Again, I miss music, can you please play music!
Robin: They are now playing music for him and/or leaving the TV on for him

My truck, my truck! Where is my truck, what happened to my truck?
Showing me a maroon, brown color pickup truck.
Aim: He had a black van, that's the only thing that I can think of that must have been lost in translation. He always worries over finances, even in his coma state.

I have lost my peripheral vision I only see like tunnel vision I only see in front of me. I don't see on the sides You need to be at the foot of my bed when you talk to me, not on my side. I can't see anything on my sides
Robin: I don't know if he had tunnel vision before he went into surgery, but his pupils are dilated but responsive to light.

(Me talking) There is a J or G around him like Jack.
Aim: Our friend Jenny (name changed for privacy reason) has been doing a lot for our family, and is close to us.
Robin: Valerie didn't place it until she said the name of the person she was with. Geirmo. Fit the J or G sound. (At his bedside that night you did the reading)

(Him talking) Again my right side is "on the spot" My left side seems non-existent. Everything revolves around my right side.

Aim: Yep, left side is pretty much non-existent right now. He can't move his left at all.

There is some talk about having me drink through a straw... Don't you dare giving me a pink one!
Aim: At this time, he was on a ventilator, and the nurses always described the amount of work the machine was doing, by that he was basically breathing out of a straw.
Robin: He is on a breathing machine and it is like he is breathing through a straw, he would not be happy if it were pink

Feels like I am taking time off to let my body heal, but I am very much aware.
There is an odd "ding" sound besides the classic medical apparatus and beeps and sounds. A "ding" sound, like a small bell.
Aim: Exactly how the ventilator sounded.
Robin: The ding and the sounds are the machines he is hooked up to right now

If you are patient, I can be too. I am just waiting for my body to repair itself, but I am here. I can't leave, but I know what's going on, just make sure you bring music, things for me to see in front of me.

He's showing me a defibrillator. Feels like he has been shocked. Code blue. Feels like I have been brought back. I was given for dead.
Robin: He also stopped breathing, which is why he has a ventilator. Hence the defibrillator and code blue. I don't know if they had to revive him, or not but he was close to dying.
Aim: He stopped breathing one morning. It was at like 5:30 or 6.

He was blue, and I thought he was dead. I thought that was it. I went out in the hallway, and I could actually see him (mentally), go out in the hall just outside the door, and felt him say he couldn't leave me yet. Then he was gone, and minutes later the Dr called me back to tell me he was ok. Maybe I'm just crazy though lol!

I am at peace; I just need to be entertained.

He is showing me glasses with no rims. He wants to make sure his glasses are around. Seeing must have been an issue too because he insists he has peripheral vision loss.
That really annoys him.

He keeps bringing images of soldiers in the desert, becomes emotional with those.
He is again showing me this young blond lady with a ponytail.
Aim: I am not too sure if she is a nurse or if she is wearing a uniform of some sort not quite sure, my friend was wondering if it was maybe about me because I've remained pretty strong throughout all of this.

There is a V also around him.
Robin: His sister's name is Valerie, the V reference. (Both V and G were at his bedside the night you did the reading)
Aim: His sister Valerie was visiting him every day, and was actually there the night you did the reading.

I hear he says 2 months. I don't know what it means; I am just hearing it.
Robin: The doctors are kind of at a loss and have given him 2 months to live, if he doesn't pass sooner.

If I come back who's going to help me fish with my right side problem?
Robin: He is an avid fisher. Something I did not know about him at all!
(Dustin's sister told Robin after she could not validate that point that Dustin indeed loved fishing)

There better be a damn good reason for me to come back because I hate having people doing things for me, I dislike this movements that you make me do right now. Moving my legs. I am not a child.
Aim: That is totally Dustin. He doesn't like anyone doing things for him ever. They were moving his legs doing the range of motion so he wouldn't get tense.

What's happening on Tuesdays and Fridays?
Tuesday and Friday, Tuesday and Friday he keeps repeating that.
Aim: I was leaving every Tuesday, and coming back Fridays. Crazy!

(Me talking) I can sense some anger here. Anger is good.
(Him talking) This place where I am at is boring; I need more stimulation. I need images on the wall, I need sounds, I need voices and I need life around me. It's too quiet.
I am not going to do anything if all I stare at is a white wall (more like light green though).
Aim: With the ugly lighting in his room there, the walls did look greenish!

I want to come back, I am a fighter, but I am going to be pissed off, I must tell you.

Robin: The entire "tone" of the reading screams Dustin, he is a bit of a grump, can seem cold and unemotional.

(Me talking) I keep being shown his upper quadrant (like liver area).
I feel like I am poisoning myself.
Something needs to be done in that area.

I keep seeing something attached to one of his big toe. Did you attach a bell or something in case he'd be moving? There is something going on with one toe. Or a toe moving.
Robin: He wiggles his toe and that night you did the reading, Valerie was massaging his feet.

Who is Patty?
He says I met Patty.
And it was fun.
Aim: I JUST found out who Patty is. I was sharing the reading with a close friend, and coworker of Dustin. His dad was also at the U then for cancer, and having surgery as well. His mom is also gifted in connecting with people outside of this life, and her name is Patty!

2 areas need to be repaired, my liver or upper quadrant something's not right and something in my brain. But my kidneys are also affected.

Energy jumped out.

Back to the bed. Again, I am seeing as if I (Isabelle) am lying on this bed seeing the foot of the bed. That's all I see. I don't see my arms; I don't see my torso. And I see the foot of the bed and nothing else.

He is REALLY making me feel like he is tired of waiting in a room that has no stimuli.
He needs sounds, colors, music.

I want music; give me music. There has to be a better way than just wait he says.
He is a proactive guy. He wants to find solutions himself.
Aim: Totally true to Dustin's personality.

He's showing me a man on a motorcycle.
I have no idea why but I am giving it to you as it comes to me.
I feel like though somehow he and the man on the motorcycle are related.
The man on a motorcycle is wearing black and it's dark outside, there are lots of lights around him.

It feels like the scene of an accident.
The man on the motorcycle feels like he's been projected in the air. There is severe trauma.
Robin: His sister thinks that the motorcycle was a reference to a friend who was injured or killed, but she wasn't certain. She also said it could be a reference to him being hit by a car when he was younger.
Aim: Dustin had a very close friend in high school. He moved to Florida, and became a motorcycle cop out there. He was chasing a suspect at night, and crashed. He died at the scene due to severe trauma.

I am back in the hospital bed. And I am cussing! F... F... F....
Aim: Again, this is totally Dustin

13

It feels like there is a disinterest from the medical team around me, like there is no real try.
Robin: The doctors are kind of at a loss and have given him 2 months to live, if he doesn't pass sooner.
And I keep hearing "bring it on" Bring the sounds and the colors and the people and movement and non-stop stimuli. This is how things get repaired.
But something needs to be done with my right side.
Aim: There was a disinterest from the medical team! They gave up on him after a week! They held a family meeting, and told us they didn't think he would make it another week.

Energy jumped out again.

When you work on me, stay in front of me, I can't see nor hear on the sides.

I am sorry I have to put you through this. Doesn't let much emotion touch him, pretty tough guy.
Very few things (seem) to affect him to the point he could pass for someone being cold.
And he thinks everyone should toughen up in a general manner.
Somehow he keeps his distance from emotions, he's scared of them.
Robin: The entire "tone" of the reading screams Dustin, he is a bit of a grump, can seem cold and unemotional.
Aim: This is very much Dustin. He never lets his emotions show.

But in his own way, he says thank you for your patience.
I am trying my best, keep working but address the points above please.

*Robin: There is SERIOUS validation for her and her family.
Aim: By the way Dustin's progress is definitely coming along since we gave him what he needed. He taps his foot to the music, to the beat! He has regained control of his right arm (he lost movement from his whole body after a long seizure) and he pulled out his tracheotomy tube the other night! Thank you so much again; you are amazing! Oh and yes, your reading gave us a lot of insight and comfort."*

Sadly a few months after our incredible connection, the cancer came back full force and Dustin released his soul to the light.

But the connection we had and the Love and Knowledge that were shared during this incredible open channel created a spark of hope for this family, knowing that Dustin had been heard and was given what he wanted before going to the light was a big relief in the process of accepting his passing.

This experiment left such an impact on me that it inspired me to write a song about Dustin and his journey. My friend and award winning film composer Dani Donadi from Donadi Music Productions composed the song. I called it "Can you hear me?"

My other passion is singing and when Dani sent me this beautiful melody one night, the lyrics poured out of my soul like a deliverance rain over the African bush after a long hot and dry summer.
This music had to tell the story of Dustin, and I wrote the lyrics in one evening.

The emotion that transpired from the lyrics was palpable and it was even hard for me to keep singing; tears (of sadness and joy at the same time) were rolling down my cheeks!

Today the song has been produced and released in the iTunes store and other platforms. Part of its proceeds will be going to raise awareness about patients in a coma or patients with Alzheimer who are not capable of expressing themselves in an aware manner.

This song tells how on the contrary of what had been thought for the longest time, our brain does not dictate the full capacity of our Consciousness and we can still communicate with our loved ones even if they don't show any medical sign of acknowledgement.
 This song wants to bring awareness on the fact that one should never ever give up because the deep connection we have with one another does not depend on our physical ability to show it. It exists no matter what and the channels are open and flowing.
(It can be found on iTunes under the name Zaza for the artist, title "Can you hear me?". A French version also exists with the title "M'entendez-vous?")

All we have to do is <u>reach out to the signal line, grab it and listen!</u>

Love and Light are the driving forces of our lives. They might even be the same thing!

It seems like our brain reduces the ability to disperse light and love around us.

It might explain why there are still so much negative energy on Earth and so many wars.
We have to filter what we receive through a machine which capacity is limited. And sometimes that machine is not wired right. Sometimes its chemical imbalances make the individual do terrible things that are clearly going away from that Love.
Sometimes illnesses and diseases disable the machine and communication, as we know it, becomes impossible.

And yet, <u>if we can bypass our brain, and reach out to our Consciousness in its purest form</u>, it seems as if the connection we have with our loved ones becomes exponentially strong and beautiful.

Dr Joe O'Connell, a very well respected Emergency Medicine Physician and speaker at the annual After Life Awareness Conference, believes that this represents a case that should be studied, replicated because the case of Dustin cannot remain an N of 1 case!

"I am a Board Certified Emergency Medicine Physician and have long been very active in study and research of what is commonly referred to as paranormal activity, specifically with regards to the "survival of consciousness"; and peri~ and post ~transitional communication. In my personal as well as medical capacity and practice I have had numerous experiences with such communication.

I chaired a panel presentation in June 2013 at the 3rd Annual AfterLife Awareness Conference* (and will this year as well) wherein we specifically discussed various ways to

Consciously be aware spiritually as well as physically, of The Soul Consciousness operating in integration with the human bio-physical brain and form as well as apart from that form independently.

The goal was to help Medical and Healthcare workers, Hospice and Chaplains to be more aware of and to help facilitate a souls' crossing over, as well as to maintain "conscious connection" with that patient throughout and beyond that process.

Concerning the dynamics in hospital settings especially in the Emergency Department as an extraordinary stressful and fast paced "event horizon", we need to focus on a new paradigm of medical "care" in viewing death not as a meaningless end of our Conscious being, "life", albeit a cessation of our integrated interdependent biophysiological existence. The new paradigm being to <u>see the 'death" event as a transitional event,</u> with a goal towards transformation of traditional medical thought and practice into an awareness of, and cooperative alliance with a peaceful and beautiful process of dying, during which maintaining an awareness of not only the survival, but thriving of <u>Energetic Soul Consciousness beyond it's biophysical disengagement.</u>

On November 8th, 2012 I had the pleasure of reviewing Isabelle Chauffeton Saavedra's amazing psychic mediumistic Conscious-to-Conscious communication with a comatose patient three days earlier. I found her experience utterly fascinating and valuable from both a medical and psycho-spiritual perspective!

Her outstanding well documented and subsequently validated experience clearly demonstrated that while in the "coma" state, our "consciousness" our "Soul" is "associated" with its machine "the body" and its computer "the brain" but not "IT", demonstrated by the "absence" of brain based "conscious" interaction during a time of active "soul conscious" interaction with Isabelle. (Similar "ultra-real" experiences in comatose state have been reported by Academic Neurosurgeon Dr. Eben Alexander III) in perhaps a state that is more as is called "astral"/"ethereal"/ "ghostlike"...awaiting its body and/or brain to be repaired and healed as in Dustin's case, or its ultimate "leaving" and progressing through higher states.

What IS also quite fascinating is a "comatose" or "unresponsive" patient's viewpoint in 'real time'; and I dare say to the visiting family as well. Nothing can be worse as the families "keeping vigil" at bedside, neither "knowing" if their loved one is even "aware" of them nor interacting "consciously" as they normally would at home with them.

One additional part of such study might be to monitor brain activity with EEG during times of medium-patient communication, and times with and without the various stimuli that a patient such as Dustin asked for; and see if it does indeed accelerate healing in brain and/or body. It seems intuitively a great idea.

I firmly feel that Isabelle's outstanding groundbreaking work needs to be replicated in scientific studies across the world. Isabelle's experience represents an N of 1, in terms of a study value, however it clearly demonstrates a heretofore unexplored and untapped resource in psychic and medical knowledge. If multiple mediums (or possibly one medium with multiple patients as a constant) could establish contact with Comatose/Vegetative state patient's Conscious', then similarities or variable data can be compared and contrasted; and an incredible breakthrough can be made in patient care as well as Human Spiritual awareness of the validity of Survival of Consciousness.

Her experience clearly and succinctly demonstrates an extraordinary medical and humanistic value in providing "enlightened" and "aware" biophysical care in order to provide the patient with his or her needs despite an inability to physically communicate; as well as provides a "bridge" to the awareness of the continuance of Consciousness during the coma and potentially "death transition phase" into the post transitional phase...
Apart from the melded Soul-Brain Consciousness we effected in utero.

I believe Isabelle's work will one day be hailed as the first in a serious of phenomenal discovery into the truth and proof not merely of Survival of Consciousness; but moreover in the extraordinary priceless value that knowledge and "awareness" will have in bettering the human condition and medical science for decades to come!"

What is important to notice is that regardless of the upbringing, regardless or the lifestyle, regardless of the issues on hand at the moment of death; there is always a tiny spark of Love that keeps the connection open. Whether it is the Love from a mother, a wife or the Love from a dog or the Love from a child or a friend or from a passed loved one already on the other side. Love is the most powerful form of energy there is. Even the worst criminal must have some form of Love attaching him or her to Consciousness as a whole. I want to believe that. I want to believe that our brain is not responsible for our Consciousness existence but is totally responsible for our interpretation of it and our acts as humans. So when the brain is taken out of the equation, there might be a chance that Consciousness is "cleaned up".

I want to believe that because I have been given the honor to share the most amazing stories of Love I have ever known, like the story of Dustin.

Those stories validate the theory that "we are conscious in spite of our brain" (As Dr Eben Alexander III describes in his book "Proof of Heaven").

CHAPTER 2

A quest and a search prompted from beyond the grave
The case of Virginia

The request came, via email, as usual. The email was simple and clear. "Hello Isabelle, this is Steve Helm, I would like to request a reading. I want you to connect with Virginia Helm".

As usual I did not know Steve or Virginia. Nor did I know anything about their lives, whereabouts, characteristics or physical appearance.

What I did not know either was that this reading would trigger questions that Steve, a former investigator for the Utah Highway Patrol could not leave unanswered.

This is another example of an amazing story of Love that lead a grief-stricken husband onto a quest to find out what happened before his wife passed away.

Steve has accepted to share the two readings I did for him with his comments, and validations, sometimes

questions that he forwarded to me post readings.
As usual, my readings are done at a distance, in a double blind setting where my sitter does not know when I do the reading and I don't know anything about my sitter or his departed loved one.

As I sit at my computer, after meditating, I write as the perceptions come to me, and I then send the email, without editing anything except for spelling errors. Steve comments and validations that were sent to me post readings are written in italic.

This is the first reading:

"Dear Steve,

I just finished your reading, what comes below is what I received chronologically with no editing whatsoever. Please bear in mind that the signal of Consciousness is always right, but my interpretation can be wrong.

Please let me know if you want to discuss any of the following, I will be happy to answer your questions. I will now be starting an EVP session and will email you the results if any in another email.
With no further ado:

My babies, my babies... I hear my babies.
Virginia was very worried about her kids.

I am shown a woman blond/dirty blond hair mid shoulder long, very distressed, very agitated. Hyperventilating.

Not sure who this would be. Her mom fits that description. She had problems with her mom. They did not have a good relationship.

I hear bipolar, bipolar.
Virginia was diagnosed as bipolar. She did not like being labeled as bipolar.

Underlying illness. Rush of blood to the head. Pressure in the head. Then loss of consciousness.
Not sure. Maybe when she died.

Hands, keeps twisting her hands together and eating her nails.
Virginia would always twist her hands together when she was nervous.

Hands always damp, sweaty.
Questions about substance abuse but misdiagnosed.
She had a problem with alcohol.

Trapped in her brain, "I was trapped in my brain"
Everything is turning white, like ashes.
Virginia felt trapped. She knew that she had mental illness.
Some issue with blood flow again. Blood, leaving extremities and rushing to other parts.

I am shown a man with a beard and camouflage pants, white T-shirt and army cap. Not feeling good vibes about this man.
No idea who this would be.
(Note: this becomes extremely relevant in the second reading, and is associated with the substance abuse affirmation)

I am sorry, I am sorry, it was not ME. Something was wrong with my brain.
I could not control it.
She always apologized for the way that she was. It was not the REAL her.

Twisting hands and fingers again.

I am shown some electric wires, I don't know why. I am just giving it to you.
There is a S associated with her other than "Steve". S. O
No idea.
She's talking about horses, "how are my horses"
She did love horse racing.
She is not moving around, she is not showing me her surroundings; she is stuck in this empty place twisting her hands and fingers.

She was scared. The man in the beard seems to play a role in her being scared. She seems like she was hiding from someone or something and could not tell what it was about.
Someone or something had a real deep, profound, dark influence on her.
I wish I knew who this was or what happened.
(Note: Again, all this becomes clear in the second reading)

She looks agitated again like someone who's under the influence of something.

I want to crack the secret. I want to tell the truth.

There was a question that needed a yes or no answer and she is finally admitting: YES, YES, YES.
She wants to free herself from this.
Not sure what the question is. I have a couple of questions that require yes or no.
She wants to move on.

She seemed pretty self-centered in a sense that she had so much to deal with mentally and emotionally that she basically had no space for anything else.
Perfect description.

I hear and see the color RED, bright red.
Something bright red from her with some white on it. It's blurry to me but one part could be round. There is a white H on it.
That's how she wants to be remembered, by this RED object.
Not sure what this object is.

There is an A (around her).
She has a daughter named Avery.

She wants to make peace; she is looking much better now. She seems to have calmed down, from the beginning of the reading.

I hear the word sister and brown associated with sister. She still loves her; she (the sister) needs to know that.

She does have a sister and they didn't speak.

She is sorry for the pain she caused.
She knows you're the best father.

Sounds just like Virginia.

It was me, I was in a spiral. There were two things involved.
Some health issues aggravated by some substance abuse or some erratic lifestyle.
I brought it up on myself.
The man with a beard also coming back. He has a dog tag.
She was diagnosed as bipolar and had a problem with alcohol.

Still no clue about the man with the beard.

F again is coming, Franck, Fred...

I see an object that is bronze color, with a white round sort of pearlish thing on top of it and a smaller one below.
It's to her right side. I don't know what it means but I feel like it's something that would be recognized; she is showing it to me for you to acknowledge I am connecting with her.
Her daughter passed away in 2005 and I placed her Urn in the casket with Virginia on her right side.

I don't feel like she went anywhere very far in her life (I mean physically) I don't see her leaving the area where she was born. It's either that or again the feeling of being stuck. But at this point, she looks liberated so I feel it has more to do with her.
She did feel stuck in life. She felt like a failure.

She had a complex of not being smart. She was craving for love and attention but was rejecting anyone who would try to give it to her because she thought she was not worth it. That includes rejecting the people who loved her the most and even children.
She did feel that way.

She did not feel she was worth being a mother, worth being anything really but yet she acted up like everything was due to her. She was suffering tremendously inside.
Again, there was some brain issue, chemical imbalance or substance abuse, something was affecting her brain tremendously and also some blood or blood flow issue.
Her feelings exactly. She was suffering.

Cold hands, damp hands...
She has not moved forward, she is waiting for forgiveness.
I forgive her.

She liked silver better than gold!
Very true. She hated gold.

I hear the word cigarettes. No more cigarettes, please she says!
She hated cigarettes.

There is a watch that was left on a nightstand, a nightstand that is to the left side of the bed.
The nightstand on the left side of the bed was mine. I kept my watch there.

And with this her energy is fading....

When Steve received the reading, it raised a few questions that left him unsettled.
He had to find the answers about this strange man with a beard and camouflage pants, who seemed to come up to me each time I was getting the substance abuse feeling.

So Steve asked me for a second reading to try and get more information about this man and also from Virginia.

This is the second reading:

"As usual, it's in chronological order, not edited, written down as it comes to me...

The bearded man looks almost like one of the guys from YMCA band with sideburns.
He's leaning on a wall. He's wearing camouflage pants, white sleeveless T-shirt and a hat like an army cap, a dog tag. But he is NOT in the army. I don't know if he's ever been. It's just a look.
He has dark hair.
But he has so much beard and hair, he almost looks like a caricature.

I see him traveling through a pretty dry area with some dry hills or mesas. He's driving an old classic convertible in fair condition.

He's a loner.

With him, it's "business as usual". I don't feel any love or sexual relationship between the two at all (Virginia and him)

But Business.

It's odd, it's very odd.
The whole persona is odd.
He appears like an odd, idealistic, loner that preys on weak and depressed women with the promise of a better world.

Almost like a self-proclaimed modern guru. I really, really don't like this vibe that I am feeling. She almost fell for it, but turned back. But he had her under his influence for a couple of weeks I would say.

There must have been some change in her behavior in a period of time I'd say about within 6 months before she passed that you could recognize during which she was seeing this guy, but again, there was nothing going on between them. He was just a weirdo.

I think she made him appear to me to show me how desperate she was.
She would have done anything in those manic moments, the craziest the better, just to push herself the furthest down she could.

It feels like she intentionally was pushing the limits, again in an effort of self-punishment...

I don't really understand this. What business did they conduct? Where did she meet this guy, how did he come into her life and how was she involved with him, if it wasn't sexual? One of the questions that I had asked her, which she replied in the first reading with Yes, YES, YES was "did you cheat on me". Why was she afraid of this guy and what dark influence did he have on her? Or, was she just afraid that I would find out about him? Did he come to my house or did she meet him somewhere else? How did she almost fall for it? Was she going to leave me for him?
(Note: All this became very clear to Steve later on)

She must have been carrying tons of guilt. She was detached emotionally because of the guilt she was carrying. In a way everything that she was doing was a form of subtle suicide, little by little.
I don't think I told you this. Virginia did commit suicide. She had attempted suicide several times. The last 6 months before she died, she would throw things at me. She would try to push me into a physical altercation with her. I did have to take her to the ground several times to get her to stop. She would cut her wrists with a knife and she eventually succeeded. She had a lot going on inside her that she would never share.

I sense something was wrong with Virginia's heart. A valve. There was either a valve malfunction or a hole. I am going with the hole. She must have had some dizzy spells, and feeling palpitations. Again she is showing me cold in extremities.
The heart was pumping more because of the problem in order to bring the blood to the different organs. I hear congenital.

31

Virginia thought she had a blood sugar issue. She would get light headed and need to eat. She did have dizzy spells and her feet were always cold. She told me on several occasions that she felt pain in her heart. It was never diagnosed.

There was also lots of anxiety and panic attacks, which could mimic a heart attack. But in her case, I think she had an underlying condition as well.
Virginia did suffer from anxiety and did have panic attacks a lot.

I am seeing a young girl with a jean jacket wearing braided pigtails like a Native American rocking something that's large rectangular and flat and white with a dark contour. I have no idea what this is. But the young lady who's rocking looks to the right and she seems absorbed in her thoughts. She's actually smiling.

Virginia's daughter, Avery is 14. She has dark black hair and has worn it in ponytails. Avery and Virginia were always close until about 7 months before she died. Avery told her that she never wanted to see her again and she called her several ugly vulgar names that I won't repeat to you.

This young girl looks like she is in her teens.

She says she is linked to the red object. It looks like a red heart that has a lace contour. And some embroidery on it. I still feel an H.
Virginia made crafts all the time. I believe that she mad a heart that fits that description. I don't know where it is or who might have it. I think it says Helm on it.

I hear Virginia is insisting I say "I could not save her, so I did not deserve to live". There is a sense that Virginia thought that if she acted differently she could have saved her daughter.
I hear the word Bella.

Virginia's youngest daughter that passed away in 2004 was named Ella. She was sick with Strep A and Virginia found her in her bed. Virginia said those exact words to me. She always thought that she could have done something differently that would have saved her. She punished herself for this.

The young girl appears again and tells me "this is the way I would look today". It looks like what she is rocking could be a large white wooden swing, the kind that people have on their porch.

There must be a cherished object that Virginia had in the form of a heart with lace trim that links her to her passed daughter.

It's not your fault; nothing is your fault. It's what my life was supposed to be she tells you.
I have felt some guilt. I have felt that if I had done something differently, I could have saved her.

There were good moments, she mentions.
Is there a joke with some boots or shoes that had to be lined up? Who is the neat freak, obsessive-compulsive person who likes everything to be in its place???
I would always just kick my shoes off and Virginia would step on them or kick them as she walked and call them "big

33

Claude shoes". She always had everything in its place and had shoes all lined up.

"She's busting your chops" saying you still have a hard time with organization.
I am still the same way.

She has a very beautiful laugh. She laughs like a child. In many ways, she was still a child and needed lots of protection and attention and would throw tantrums like a child.
That is one of the things I miss the most about her is her laugh. It was contagious. She had the most beautiful smile. It lit up my world.

No more tantrums, she jokes.
She would throw tantrums. Violent tantrums. I hated that. It was usually when she was drinking. Otherwise, (she was) very sweet.

I am so happy here.
I am so relieved that she is happy. I knew she would be, as her spirit is free from all of her illnesses and addictions.

Did you keep her toothbrush for a while after she passed? She is showing me two toothbrushes in the same glass.

I did not keep her toothbrush. But I did keep my old toothbrush when I bought a new one. There are two toothbrushes in the same glass where we kept our toothbrushes.

Now she is showing me around a house. In the living room, I am facing a fireplace. It's brown maybe with a wood mantle. To my left I have two windows. It's not very bright in the room there is a sofa to the left and a sofa table in front of it, its side to the fire place. There is an object on the mantle to the left that is of significance for her. A photo? It's blurry to me but it's like a spot of off white color, oval shape. To my right I go to the kitchen, there is another room in between but it's open space and I don't know what that is.
She just wanted me to acknowledge the object on the mantle.
I am living with my parents. In their basement, there is a couch with the side facing the fireplace. It is not very bright down there, as it is below ground. There are two windows to the right if you are facing the fireplace. There is a stand next to the fireplace that holds photos. In that stand there is a picture of us taken the day before our wedding. She is wearing her white wedding dress. It is not oval though.

Do you have gravel in your driveway? I hear the sound of gravel. I walk there sometimes.
She is making me feel she has seen you sitting on a chair next to a table that would look like a dining table your face turned towards a window to your
left thinking of her and there is some sort of chest or curio chest behind you.
She was there when this happened or when this happens, as it seems it has happened more than once.
There is no gravel in my driveway, but she walked a lot. The chair at the dining table is where I sit for dinner at my parents' house.
I face the window. There is a curio behind me where I sit.

I often stare out the window and think about her while I eat. My youngest son asked me one time what I was looking at, because I was just staring out the window, lost in thought. This does happen quite often.

You need to open the window and let the light inside your house she says!
It has double meaning.
She's absolutely right, but I don't know how. I miss her so much. I have never loved anybody like I love her. She was truly my best friend.

She wants you to free yourself; she is fine.
I know that I need to do this, but again, I don't know how. I need to figure that part out.

All that she has shown me was to make sure you understood that it was her, as I did not know her and she needed to convey who she was, but she says, now this is over, this is no longer me.
I can move on now because I have been able to tell you that it was only me and no one else's fault.
I am thankful that she is now at peace. All I have ever wanted was to make her happy. She is finally happy. I know that at times, I contributed to her feeling worthless. I have asked her for forgiveness for any mean thing I have ever said to her, or for any time that I didn't do enough as a husband, that made her feel unloved.

After all it's all within Love and Light... She's fading away. And with this I close the séance.

I am so thankful to you, Isabelle. I know for a fact that you have contacted Virginia and that you have connected me to her through your unbelievable gift. I cried last night because of the freaky guy in her life.

I cried last night because I was happy that she was free from this secret. I forgive her.

I also cried because I miss her terribly and want her back.

I hope that I am reunited with her in the hereafter, whatever that is.
I woke up at 2 am and I had the chills. I felt like she was there. I did not hear anything or see anything, but I felt like she was there with me.
I really didn't know what to think about all of this. I am convinced that you are for real. I consider you a friend now. I have shared some of the most intimate parts of my life with you even though you are the one that saw it. All I did was confirm it. You are awesome. Thank you. I am attaching some pictures for you, but I'm sure you have already seen her face."

A couple of weeks later, to my surprise, I received this email:

"Hello Isabelle,
I just wanted to update you on the guy with the beard from Virginia's reading. It has really been bothering me. I asked a friend of mine who still lives in Oklahoma, where she died, to go to the liquor store and see if there was somebody that works there that matches that description. He immediately told me that he got the chills. He said that he knows a guy that matches that description works there. He said he reminds him of Yosemite Sam. He said that he sold that guy a TV and that he gave a girl that works with him the creeps.

He went to the liquor store and asked the owner where that guy was. The owner said that he fired him because he was giving away alcohol off the shelf and was trying to take girls to his house. Now I know where Virginia was getting her alcohol.

I just wanted to let you know what I found out.

I hope your weekend has been good."

It always amazes me how our loved ones in pure energy form can be so insistent in bringing forth information that apparently makes no sense. When I receive a feedback that says: "I have no idea what you are talking about", well let's be honest, it's a little embarrassing. Though it happens very rarely, when it happens, I have to remember that I KNOW how to classify and differentiate the information I receive. I have been trained by the best to do that.

I have indeed learned to recognize the types of information I can trust and the types that I have to be wary about. And yet, when a piece of trusted information does not seem to be validated by a sitter, there is not much to say other than: "There is more to it, maybe it's not obvious now, but there is more to it".

Therefore it is thanks to people like Steve who go the extra mile to research, find out, and compare notes that our work gets its full recognition.
In the case of Virginia, that man with lots of hair, the beard and the odd character who had a dark influence

on her was real and it played a pretty big role in her addiction before she passed away.

By telling the truth post mortem, Virginia brought closure to Steve and helped solve a mystery that had plagued her husband with remorse, doubt and guilt for months.

As an established psychic medium today, this is what I work for. I strive creating protocols of connections that can be trusted as valid, based on facts, verifications and a strict code of ethics. In my readings, I incorporate notions of rigorous scientific settings, well established viewing techniques once embraced by the CIA and DIA and self taught perception processes to further validate the connections I create.

How do I know that the connection I made with Dustin, the comatose man, is true?
How am I so sure that the emotions I felt and the facts I stated in Virginia's case can be trusted as real?

   It took me years, a lot of learning, a lot of detours to come to this. From self teaching to taking courses in Controlled Remote Viewing with the best in the field, it all started 45 years ago…

CHAPTER 3

Welcome to Earth

On a beautiful evening of early spring 1968, in a rather small town, in Normandy, France, a midwife came out of the delivery room and showed my dad my little body all swaddled in a white blanket. Ultrasound equipment did not exist at the time, so it was always a surprise as to what the sex of the baby would be.

When my dad nervously asked the nurse: "So, is it a boy?" she opened the blanket and said: "What do you think that is?"
My parents were already blessed with a beautiful twelve-year old daughter who also desperately wanted a little brother.
My dad who always spoke his mind, and still does, looked at my little naked body and loudly let go of a: "S***t", another girl"!

That was the beginning of my life, a defining moment that clearly set the path for me.

I was not a boy but my dad had set his mind on one and he had already planned that I would be an engineer or a scientist, because there was no other way. Had I been a boy, which is what he was hoping for, that's what he had already in store for me.

I had the most amazing childhood a child can dream of. Loving parents, a big sister who loved being a tomboy and loved animals so much she became a veterinarian and the most incredible extended family with lots of uncles and aunts and cousins.

I came late in the picture, though. My sister was twelve years old when I was born and I did not have any cousins my age apart from a third degree cousin I was seeing during summer vacations sometimes.

My childhood was spent playing a lot by myself as my dad had just started his own business and my mom was helping him. They always dedicated ample time to oversee my homework and make sure it was done. My dad also felt like he had to give me extra math lessons every single day of my life, as he considered math the key language to success in life. But for playing, I was on my own.

My first memory of intense connection with some idea or concept was when I was five.
I was always playing outside in the garden and I was always imagining myself being a Native American. But I was born and raised in France! Where did this come from?

I would ask my paternal grandfather who lived on the same land in another house to make me bows and arrows and build me teepees. I would always ride imaginary horses and defend "my people" against the "cowboys".

I guess I was so into character that my parents got me the most incredible gift that year for Christmas. It was a western wagon with a plastic horse and a pedal system. I would sit in the wagon and use the pedals. The horse would pull and I'd go everywhere with it in the garden. It was all about the American West. Arizona was written in big black letters on the side of the white plastic cover that simulated the cloth fabric used around a wagon.

Next thing I know, when all the girls my age in school wanted to be princesses for Mardi Gras (our Halloween, before Halloween became popular in France too), I wanted a Native American costume and loved wearing it all the time with my bear teeth necklace, boasting my plastic tomahawk at invisible enemies.

I felt connected with the Native American nations, I felt like I knew them.

I did not know at the time that it was the beginning of a journey that would take me across the Atlantic Ocean in search of that connection. A connection that later, I would understand, was going to go beyond the Native American culture, beyond being human. But I had to go through all the steps my life would take me into first, to make that connection.

CHAPTER 4

Learning to be me

Back in France, life with my family was happy. Life outside the family cocoon was miserable.

My very first day at kindergarten was my very first experience with bullying and it would not stop until age thirteen. I was very chubby as a little girl but very outgoing because in my family it was all about being yourself and laughing and embracing life. This did not fit well with a couple of girls in class who made it clear to me they were going to make my life miserable for the rest of the elementary period and beyond.

You see, my dad, an engineer and a mathematics addict, had already taught me numbers and additions and my mom had already been through the reading apprenticeship with me.
So I arrived at school with "knowledge" and it set me apart immediately from the others. Kids did not like me, and even the teacher did not like me.

Since I knew the curriculum already, I remember the teacher always trying to dismiss my abilities by not allowing me to participate in class projects that would include drawing or being creative. She kept repeating to me that my drawings were not good enough. I remember this huge wall project done by the class on which I was not allowed to do anything. I was very sad.

So the more rejected I felt, the more I turned to my family and my dad to learn more academic things.

At the end of kindergarten, my dad decided that he had enough and that based on my level of knowledge and what was done in class I should be bumped up to 1st grade immediately (in France at that time, kindergarten was for 2 years. They called it "Small Kindergarten and Big Kindergarten"). He did not want me to waste one more year in Kindergarten with this teacher who clearly disliked me.

Of course the Kindergarten teacher refused saying that based on my drawings (you've got to laugh at that one) I was not mature enough to move up; but I knew how to read, write and count when the other kids did not, and apparently that did not measure up in the balance.

I was not aware of the big fight that ensued after that between my dad and the principal. All I remember is one day, my mom took me to school to a different building and she said that a lady would spend a few hours with me to test my counting and reading level and other things. My mom was not allowed in the tiny room where I sat with this lady and I remember being scared at the beginning.

But then everything turned into a game. I had to count bars, and to remember where she had hidden keys and next thing I know, my dad is telling me "you are going to 1st grade!"

I guess the psychologist did not really care about my drawings!

[By the way this is one of my later paintings (at age 23) of my beloved English Setter Rocky. I should have mailed it to my kindergarten teacher! Not that it is a masterpiece, far from it, but I believe I made a few progress since the art critics of my kindergarten's teacher.]

So here I am in first grade, free from the bullies (as they stayed in kindergarten), or so I thought.
I forgot that at recess time everyone was mixed to play together.

The better I became academically, the more bullied I was and the bigger I was becoming.

I ended up ballooning in an obese manner at age twelve, still bullied, still top of my class.

During all these years, at home, it was all about being the best, and the first and not caring about what the others said. So I was going through my daily math lessons with my Dad, including vacation days and off days and national days.

At nights I would often, before going to bed, go outside in the garden and look up at the sky. I was fascinated. I felt like this was so beautiful, it filled me with the love and acceptance I desperately wanted from the others and I did not get. (Again, not from my family, I was very much loved there)

I could not explain what I felt but I could stay hours looking up. So of course my Dad taught me the constellations and started buying books on astronomy.

When I was seven, one night, my dad said: " hop in the car". This was very out of character and very unusual. It was past bedtime!
" I have something to show you", he said.

So we drove half way to the next little medieval town. We stopped at the highest point on the road, on top of a high hill, in a field.
We got out of the car and stood there looking at the sky.
It was a beautiful starry night, filled with twinkling dots shining through the very immaculate dark sky. No air pollution back then in the 70's, especially in the countryside.

I remember a light breeze brushing my cheeks and hair and this sensation of excitement that only a child can feel. My entire body was electrified and shaking with anticipation.
"What are we doing here Dad", I asked.

My dad kept looking at his watch and kept saying: "it's going to happen soon."

"But what is going to happen?" I retorted.

"You will see, be patient…"

I had no idea why we were there but I knew that my dad would have not brought me to this special place if it hadn't been for something important. And that thought kept feeding my excitement and amplifying my level of anticipation.

And then suddenly he said: " Look, you see this bright light moving in the sky?"
So I looked up and saw a fairly large brilliant dot moving across the sky, like a never ending shooting star and I said: "yes, I see it, what is this?"

"Ma Cherie, you are witnessing an historical moment," he said.
"You are looking at Apollo and Soyuz, two satellites (one American and one Soviet) that have joined each other in space and are moving as ONE for the first time right before your eyes"

I was in awe!

The connection I felt with the Universe(s) at that moment was immense and intense. I somehow understood I was part of something so big and so beautiful it was overwhelming.

It was about at the same time that I started to have trouble falling asleep. I did not have night terrors with horrible nightmares, no. I just had a very hard time letting go of the "light". I felt, there was a presence in my room, I felt that I was being watched.
I kept ending up in my parents' bedroom and bed "because there was someone in my room". Though my parents tried to rationalize and explain to me that there was no one in my room, I still felt the presence.

I felt so bad coming to my parents' bed almost every night that one night I just packed my pillow and my blanket and silently came to their room and made a makeshift bed at the foot of theirs. I would have slept everywhere but in my bedroom.

Needless to say that the next morning, when my dad woke up and almost fell, tripping over me in the dark, he was not too happy!

    Little by little I learned how to control the fear and I accepted the presence. It never really went away but I got used to it and lived with it.

CHAPTER 5

My first brush with Death

One day, during summer vacations in the center of France, I was with my mom buying souvenirs for the family. In summer my mom, dad, my sister and I would always visit different regions of France with the little RV that my parents had bought.

Those vacations were absolutely fantastic. It was always about discovering new things, learning our country's history in a fun way, which I loved to do, and being with the people I loved the most, my family!

That day, I wanted to buy a can of specialty food from the region we were in for my maternal grandfather (a kid's idea of a great souvenir!). I knew he loved that specific dish and I was very excited at the idea of seeing his smile when I would give him the can upon our return home.
But instead of giving me a soft smile like she would usually do, marveling at my child's silly loving request, my mom became somber.

She tried to explain to me that it might not be the best idea for my grandfather. But I insisted, because I did not understand why it would not be the best idea; that was his favorite food!
My mom gently tried again to explain that my grandfather was sick and that he might not appreciate this type of food this time around. But in my child's mind I did not understand. It did not make sense.
I kept saying: "It's ok, when he feels better he will love to have it."
In front of so much insistence from my part, my mom decided to let go and let me buy the can with my little savings.

When we came back home a few days later, I remember feeling a sense of darkness coming over my parents and my family.
We had to rush to my uncle's house, where my maternal grandfather was living. Everyone was here. It was late in the evening and dark outside and inside the house too.
I insisted to take the can of food with me. I was so excited to surprise my grandfather with his favorite food. My mom did not say anything and let me take it.

There was a lot of people coming and going from and to my grandfather's bedroom. And I kept saying "but I want to give him his can". I had it in my hands.
At one point my mom, took me by my shoulders and said "Ma Cherie, your grandfather is too sick, you cannot give him his can of food right now".
I was so disappointed. I did not understand. On top of everything I was not even allowed to see him.

I remember feeling so sad and not understanding the bustling in and out of his bedroom. I felt like: "why can't I go see him? Everybody is going to see him."

My grandfather and I also shared a little secret. He used to keep a chocolate bar in his chest drawer and whenever I visited he would always take me to his room with his finger across his lips, prompting me to be very silent. He would always whisper to me: "shhh do not tell anyone, it is a secret between you and I" and would give me a square of his chocolate bar, pretending it was a state secret that had to be guarded no matter what! Nobody could know he was hiding chocolate there and by sharing it with him, I was bounded to secrecy!

Not being able to enter his room to give him his favorite food and share our little secret was making me very sad. As a child the only thing that mattered was the loving bond that I had with him and no one or nothing was supposed to interfere with it or destroy it.

The next day, I was in the kitchen with my mom, when all of the sudden my dad came and said something to her. She dropped everything and left.
I was told my grandfather had just passed away.

You see, my grandfather passed away from lung cancer and I understand now the last moments of his bodily existence might not have been suitable to watch for such a young and sensitive girl that I was.

I was not allowed either to go pay my last respects on his funeral day.

In order to protect me from the reality of death, my parents did not realize that they had just planted in me the very seed that would gradually make me who I am today.

I started to wonder what death was all about and why it was so secret and so sad; why even if sick, my grandfather was not given the joy to get his favorite food. I felt cheated and I felt he had been cheated. I was angry and at the same time did not understand what was going on.

But instinctively though I felt already that it was not about the gift to him, but about the LOVE; I loved my grandfather and I wanted him to know it; the only way I knew to show him my affection was by giving him the can I had bought for him with my own savings!

And now it was too late!

Then I heard people saying that he was at peace, in heaven. So I started to question around about that.

That's when I was explained about God, my first real brush with the concept. I had of course heard of Jesus before and the golden rules but had never linked him with God and his (her) super power.

I was born and raised Catholic. I had been baptized when I was a baby but never showed any interest in the matter; this is why my parents, unlike for my sister who did her Communion, gave me the choice to go to church school or not. I chose not to.

After my grandfather's passing, while people were trying to reassure me that he was "resting in peace" my dad, the math person, did not agree with that view. He kept saying, that when we die, this is it. We no longer exist. There is no such thing like heaven.

This was extremely confusing and did not answer my questions either way. Will my grandfather ever get my can of food or not? Will he ever know that I was there that night behind the door wanting so bad to talk to him about this delicious can of food I had especially bought for him? And who is that God who takes my grandfather away from me without letting me see him and talk to him anyway. Why do we have to "rest in peace", it's like sleeping in the dark, and I hated that. And if there is no heaven and death is the end, where is my grandfather now?

So many questions and neither answer from God, nor from science.

So I turned to what I knew would make me feel good. I turned to the sky.
And I looked up that night and let myself fly into this beautiful starry sky the way I was used to. To me it was like watching an inspiring painting, listening to an amazing symphony at the same time.

I started to wonder and ponder. If we are so tiny, if the Universe(s) is so big and capable of creating so much beauty and giving me so much joy and love just by immersing myself into it, there is no way that death be the end of it, and no one is waiting to be saved by a

God, we are just part of something big that we can't grasp. We are all safe, we are all just One.

My dad once told me about the notion of infinite space and it had had a profound impact on me. Grasping the notion of infinite was so mind blowing. But now somehow, looking at the sky and at all these stars and the darkness (a reassuring darkness, not a scary one) as far as I could see was giving me a sense of hope that somewhere in this infinite space my grandfather was alright.

I was ten years old.

From that moment, it became clear to me that there was "something else", something else beyond science and religion, something religion had failed explaining to me and something I felt science was far from being able to do yet.

But somehow I felt that all the answers about life and death that I needed so badly were hidden in this dark, starry night sky right in front of me.

I was set on my path and declared from that point on that I wanted to become an astronomer when asked what I wanted to do when I grew up.

As I started researching the field and curriculum needed to become an astronomer, I quickly realized that there were only about four jobs allotted in public observatories in France every year and rethought my choice.

Yes I was only ten but figured, I am good but I am probably not good enough to make it to one of this 4 positions (I can't believe I was reasoning like that!). So I then declared I wanted to do research and be an astrophysicist. (I would still get to watch the sky but go even deeper; it was perfect.)

From that point, anything even remotely close to astronomy, astrophysics, science and energy had become a focus of my curiosity.

I started to get interested in Spiritism and table tipping very quickly. When I was seeing my third degree cousin on vacations, my favorite thing to play with him was thought transference and telepathy. I would take four cards and have him pick one and think about it so that I could guess it.

I became sort of obsessed by the idea of an undiscovered energy that was linking us all and had the power of transferring data and thoughts and moving objects too.

My mom is a very intuitive person. She is also hyper sensitive. She would very commonly know things before they would happen; she'd know who was calling before picking up the phone. But she never "worked" the muscle to use it as I call it. So in a way I guess she was not surprised seeing me getting interested in the subject of psi and ESP.

My dad, the scientist could not fathom the idea that "spirits" existed but remained open to the concept of undiscovered energy.

CHAPTER 6

Connecting with energy for the first time consciously

At age twelve, I had become so obsessed by it all, that while having a family gathering at my uncle's house, I could not stop talking about it during dinner. My dad got so tired of it that he stood up and said: "That's it! I have had enough of this nonsense, I am going to prove once for all that all this is just pure illusion"

He asked my aunt if she had a wooden round table, which she did.

My dad enrolled my sister (who was twenty four at the time and also very much interested in the idea) and the three of us went to the dark living room of my uncle's house. Everyone else remained in the kitchen, door closed.

My uncle's house is an old house that has been an ongoing remodeling project for as long as I can remember.
The living room of this house is a long rectangular

room where two very large tables can fit the whole family when we are all gathered. It was built around a well that pre-existed and my uncle decided to keep the well during the construction of the room as an added décor item.

Imagine sitting around a small round table in a large dark room with no one else than your sister and your dad.
On one end of the room, an oversized fireplace is standing casting a large shadow on the back wall.
Next to it, on the floor, there is a wooden hatch that leads to the ancient cellar of the house.
On the yard side, four French doors with multi pane windows cover the entire length of the wall creating a giant opening to the darkness outside.

All you see are the faces of your dad and sister dancing in the light of the unique candle placed on the table.

When you are twelve, it sets the emotions and the expectations high!

While my sister remained neutral, my dad clearly stated that no spirits would be invoked, as he did not believe in this "nonsense".

I did not have much choice in the bargain, but I was so excited at the idea of finally doing my very own experimental table tipping session that I immediately agreed with my dad who proceeded to add that the only approach he could have was that of a scientific one. He added he was open to the idea of manipulating a form of energy that we did not know about by asking the table to move. "But that was it".

Being the mathematics guy and the engineer that he was, my dad was in his element with the theory/experiment/proof system that he had set forth for our séance and thus felt comfortable doing it without compromising his scientific integrity.

The following rules were then stated:
No touching of the table with hands or knees or any body part
No touching each other's hand
No cheating (which to me was beyond conceivable, I could not even fathom the idea of cheating, because I knew this was real!)
Just tell the table to move, in your mind.

Fair enough.

As we proceeded to sit around the table I could start feeling my entire body quivering from excitement and from the adrenaline pumping. The energy was clearly rising at a rapid pace.
I wanted this experiment to work so badly to prove my dad, but most of all to prove myself, that I was on the right tracks!
My level of anticipation was so high that my eyes started tearing. I could hardly contain all this energy building up in my body and soul. I knew, I KNEW it was going to work, because I could feel it.
I was watching the slightest move, listening to the slightest noise or crack while I kept repeating in my mind as if I was talking to the table "Move, Move, Move, Move…."

My eyes were closed and tears kept coming down my cheeks from the flow of energy going through my body. The sensation was incredible. I had never felt such a level of emotions through my body before that moment.

Once in awhile, I was glancing at my dad and my sister to see what THEY were feeling. They both had their eyes closed and seemed pretty relaxed but focused.

I was waiting for the moment when the table would start moving so that all this accumulated anticipation could be released back into the Universe(s).

I was waiting, and waiting and keeping my focus very intense, still repeating in my mind "Move, move, move…."

All of the sudden it occurred to me that we had not specified to the table how it was supposed to move… Was it supposed to move to the right or to the left? What if my sister was asking it to move to the left and my dad to the right? That would most certainly annul the process! So I broke the concentration and the silence and told my sister and dad about my thoughts.

We all then agreed to one direction, to not "confuse" the table!

And we waited, still focused, still having the energy flowing, and waited.

After about thirty minutes, my dad let go of a long sigh and said: "well I believe this table is not going to move, so I think we should stop now."

I was devastated. I begged for a few more minutes. My older sister helped me convince my dad to continue for ten more minutes. Then he could declare the experiment a total failure if nothing was happening. He agreed.

More than ever, I went back into a deep trance. I think for the first time of my life, I learned what it was to "feel connected" with my right brain and totally "disconnected" from my left brain. I was not looking around, I was not espying for noise and cracks, I was not hoping for the table to move, I just let it go, totally, surrendering to the energy.

That is when it happened.

We heard distinct wood crack noises coming from the table, it "woke us up" from our trance like state of Consciousness and the three of us looked at each other with anticipation.
We immediately went back at it and then, before we even had time to acknowledge anything, the table, literally threw itself at my dad who only had a split second to shift his body to his left to avoid being hit. The table did not really lift itself. It dragged itself towards my dad and went crashing on the floor, breaking a wooden leg in the process.

The crashing noise was so violent that it sent the rest of the family running out of the kitchen, which was on the other side of the hallway, with people yelling "are you ok", "what happened?"

And we were just frozen there in our torpor, totally incapable of giving any answer to anyone for a few seconds, which seemed long minutes...

My dad finally said: "Well, the table fell!"
My aunt, who was an absolute skeptic, said something like: "you mean you tripped in the dark and the table fell"? (I am still trying to help her open her heart to the other side, especially now that my uncle has crossed over to the light)

" No no, we did not trip, we did not touch it, and it fell, by itself."

Everyone was gasping in disbelief except my aunt who started to laugh hysterically.
Her laugh attack was so bad she left the room to go back to the kitchen.

But the rest of the family became very intrigued and knowing the scientific integrity of my dad was not going to deny the experience.
On the contrary, it got them very excited and now, my uncle and all the cousins wanted to replicate the experiment.

But this time, because we were about twelve people we would use the kitchen table in the kitchen. The kitchen table was a very sturdy, heavy large wooden oval table. It would take two very strong men to lift it.
People were chatting, we had to send my aunt to her bedroom, she was still going at it laughing hysterically, no one was really focused like they should have been,

the level of concentration and relaxation was so low that a fly would have had more attention spam.
I knew from that point, it would not work.
The experience was doomed from the beginning.

So the whole family decided to play card instead to end the evening the way we, as a family, would always do.

But for me this experience was an absolute high in my young life of researcher in the matter of life after death and ESP.
Even if my dad did not let us enlist the help of disembodied energies, I knew we had connected with something or someone that had far more power that we thought it had. And to this day, thirty some years later, my scientific dad, now in his 80s will still admit he has no explanation for what happened that night.

This became my new forte, my new way of affirming my difference with the others.
And it got me some new friends in middle schools who wanted to know more about contacting the other side.
I would organize séances at lunch time in a room at school, using a glass from the lunch room and letters cut in paper, putting the glass in the middle of all the letters positioned in a circle on the floor or on a table: a makeshift Ouija board.

I do not have any recollection of any successful experiment using this method in school, but it built my curiosity and confidence even more.

I would not miss any occasion to suggest a séance with friends. I remember one winter my parents sent me to "winter camp" with my sister and brother in law. My brother in law was the director of the camp. It was a ski camp in the Alps with kids from thirteen to sixteen years of age.

I had been offered to come for free if I was helping in the kitchen for breakfast, lunch and dinner services everyday. I jumped at the offer and said yes of course, not without negotiating with my parents who were not convinced that I should go, even though my older sister was going to be there.

While doing my job during the day and escaping for a few ski trips and walks in the beautiful snowy countryside, I was asked one day to come up with some ideas for evening activities. Each evening there were five or six different activities to which the kids could register during the day by placing their nametags on the board listing the different interests.

Of course I offered a Ouija and table tipping séance! It was a total success within the girls, less with the guys… That night strange things happened like a candle blowing by itself and the glass moving always towards one particular girl… But even at thirteen, I had my integrity, I knew someone had cheated and I really disliked it. So when asked to do it again the following night, I declined.

After that moment I took a little step back because life got in the way. We had so much homework without even counting the extra one that my dad would always give me in mathematics that my mind was just on cruise control for school.

Then I became really fed up with being chunky so I really got serious about dieting and finally became happy in my body, which coincided with puberty and had an inversely proportional effect on my studies. The more weight I was losing, the less attention I was paying to my grades as I was finally getting the attention from the others that I had been longing for, for so many years.

But I still went on and obtained my Baccalaureate Section C (mathematics and physics). In France at the time, we had to choose a major already as a freshman in high school and I chose math and physics.

CHAPTER 7

Mind over matter? The case of Psychokinesis

The term psychokinesis is derived from the Greek words psyche, which means "soul," and kinein meaning "to move." The power of psychokinesis is the power to move things with your soul.
What is interesting to note is that Psyche was a mortal woman in Greek mythology. After marrying the son of Aphrodite, she was made a real immortal goddess by Zeus. She was always pictured with butterfly wings. Psyche went from being a mortal in a body to an immortal eternal concept of beauty and love.

In Dr. Eben Alexander III's book "Proof of heaven" he describes being transported from one point to another in the realm he had come to during his NDE on the wings of a butterfly…

The association between the butterfly and the soul makes total sense.
If you think of a caterpillar, stuck in its earthly body, not able to do much, other than to meet its own needs for food, breathing and surviving living in harmony, it

pretty much depicts us as humans, trapped in a body that limits our capabilities as a soul.

But then comes what I call the "little death". Caterpillar no more gives "birth" to a magnificent butterfly, which can spread its wings and soar, finally free of its limitations. The "psyche" is a free entity that knows no limits. (As Psyche, the mortal that she was, turned immortal in the Greek Mythology).

In Pychokinesis, the soul has the potential to affect the physical world.

Many experiments have been done in history with a particular craze for it during the spiritualism period in Europe and in the US from the 1840s to the 1920s.
In spiritualism or spiritism, it was believed that one could communicate with "spirits" and have them materialize in ectoplasms or move objects.

Later during the Cold War, it is known that both Soviet and American governments tried to study and experiment on the phenomenon.

Psychokinesis has raised many doubts in the world of skeptics through the years because it is difficult to grasp the idea that our Soul, working through our Mind and Brain has the ability to do such things.
But it does.

There have been many modern experiments done on the matter. But I am particularly interested in two of them.
One of the most fascinating ones is the work of Masaru Emoto, a Japanese forward thinker on water. Dr Emoto

has been studying what water can reveal to us about our interaction between our souls and matter.

" Masuru Emoto is a graduate of the Yokohama Municipal University's department of humanities and sciences, with a focus on International Relations. In 1986, he established the IHM Corporation in Tokyo. In October of 1992, he received certification from the Open International University as a Doctor of Alternative Medicine. Subsequently he was introduced to the concept of micro cluster water in the US and Magnetic Resonance Analysis technology. The quest thus began to discover the mystery of water.

He undertook extensive research of water around the planet, not so much as a scientific researcher, but more from the perspective of an original thinker. At length, he realized that it was in the frozen crystal form, that water showed us its true nature. He has gained worldwide acclaim through his groundbreaking research and discovery, that water is deeply connected to our individual and collective Consciousness."
(Extract from Dr. Masuru Emoto's website)

Dr. Masuru Emoto is a Doctor in Alternative medicine. His observations and experimentations on water crystals are groundbreaking and reveal the true nature of our Soul, our Psyche.

He has shown that water crystals exposed to different type of "thoughts" change their very core crystalline structure according to the thought.
In other words, when thoughts of Love and Compassion are sent to a water crystal, it turns into a magnificent, well organized, radiant crystal. The same

results are found with classical or melodious music. When a crystal taken from the same sample of water is exposed to thoughts of hatred, violence and harsh music, or sad music, the crystal becomes totally disorganized and unable to produce a perfect structure.

Words are even "shown" to the water, which in return, creates a crystal disorganized or organized based on the type of word shown.

His experiments show that remote "prayer" by a group of people or "positive thought transference" as I like to call it creates a beautiful crystal as well.

If we, as souls, as pure energy, have the ability to act upon water, imagine what our thoughts can do to ourselves and others as our human bodies are made of up to 75% water! Imagine what we can do to our planet, which about 70% of its surface is water-covered!

A lot of damage can be done if our intentions are not of Love and Compassion.

My good friend and skeptic Nicolas, asked me, "But why in your view does the Universe(s) have to be of Love?".

Because Love makes life flow. Because in the Universe(s) creation always wins over destruction.

Across the Universe(s) the force of gravity and motion create destruction in black holes and galaxies attracting each other and colliding.

But if we look at the big picture, at the Universe(s)'s scale, gravity ultimately becomes a creator. As galaxies and galaxy clusters are pulled towards one another by gravity and collide in the most violent cosmic events, stars are ripped apart, enormous amounts of gas under tremendous pressure are ejected in all directions, but then gravity continues to work its magic and creates a more mature, a bigger galaxy with billions of new stars being born by the minute!

Gravity in a sense is a very destructive force but on a cosmic scale is a very creative power.
The forces of creation of life are always prevailing.
Gravity tends to take the Universe(s) towards a "positive creative" state.

What is Love, other than a creative force of attraction that makes life flow?

So if our intentions are not of Love, we can potentially destroy irreversibly.
Love applied to our Earthly matters tends to take our world towards a "positive creative" state.

Our Consciousness has the power to ultimately on a grand scale create our reality and give life to it. It is our driving force, literally our lifeline.

As we learn how to love others, and ourselves, we indeed create the potential for our own and others' beauty and self-healing. We also gain the power to heal our planet.
"Beauty is in the eyes of the beholder" is actually truer than we think.

***

Another interesting research has been conducted on Random Number Generators (RNG). It has been noted that a deviation from randomness can be associated with collective attention. Organizations such as Global Consciousness Project (GCP) and IONS (Institute of Noetic Sciences) have recently conducted several experiments to show that a significant gathering of people could affect a total randomly created sequence of bits. The method used is very simple, they replicate the readings of random generated bits over and over in a "control" situation at a location where nothing is happening and compare to the reading when a major physical gathering of people with a certain anticipation for an event is happening.

The random bits generated in the "control" situation show no type of organization or structure.

But the studies show clearly a peak in deviation of randomness around the "event" into some sort of structured generated sequence of bits, indicating that at the quantum level Consciousness has indeed impacted reality.

Some events such as the 9/11 tragedy or the devastating tsunami of March 2011 in Japan have created deviations in RNG readings.

The study that was conducted by IONS was about the gathering of Burning Man in 2012 a New Age event that brings more than 50 000 people in the middle of the Nevada Black Rock desert each year. The gathering gives life to all sorts of eclectic forms of arts and celebrations with a culminating point when a central structure with a giant statue of a man is burned in a joyful and cheerful manner. It might sound a little crazy but whether you call it a giant Woodstock or a living museum of folk art or a mega New Age gathering, it did produce a deviation in randomness in the study conducted by IONS.

For the sake of scientific research it does not matter what the research target is, what matter is the results. And the results are here to clearly show that at the quantum level, the emotional energy conveyed by the collective Consciousness did affect simple bits of 0s and 1s!

It also demonstrates that any type of emotional energy put out there does have an effect on reality. This is why it becomes our responsibility to create positive and loving thoughts throughout our life.

As we look through our eyes with our souls, we can create the possibility of beauty and harmony at the quantum level.

In fact, quantum physics suggest that everything in the Universe(s) has a wave - particle duality. It also suggests that observing an object affects its quality (being a wave or a particle).

To better understand Dr. Masuru Emoto's experiments, GCP and IONS experiments and how YOU can affect your life and the life of people around you and Earth and how WE are ALL CONNECTED and ALL ONE, here is a brief explanation of what happens at the quantum level.

The double slit experiment is a famous experiment that demonstrates that observing an object affects the said object and its properties.

Let's look at this experiment to understand what's going on.

First let's take electrons which are tiny pieces of matter, particles and let's bombard them into an opening made on a thin plate, called a slit. On the other side of the thin plate where the slit has been cut to let the electrons through, a screen is positioned.

As the electrons go through the slit, they leave a clear imprint on the screen of the shape of the slit, acting like normal particle would do.

Now, add a second slit to that, parallel to the first one. Shoot the same beam of electrons. One should expect to see on the screen two parallel imprints, of the shape of the slits. As the electrons arrive at the slits, some should go through the first slit and some should go through the second one randomly, or so we think, and we should obtain this clear image of two parallel lines on the screen.

Yet, it's not what's happening. On the screen appears a pattern of dark and bright bands consistent with the imprint of colliding waves (where the waves collides, they cancel each other and create a dark pattern, hence the dark bands).

Some how, in the process of adding one slit, the electrons changed their very nature of being a particle and turned into a wave!

Scientists thought that maybe the electrons going through the slits would bounce off each other on the other side, giving the impression that it had become a wave but it was not.

So they decided to "trick" the electrons and recreated the experiment by shooting one electron at a time, to avoid the bouncing theory.
They were astonished to discover that the pattern had not changed; it would still create after hours of shooting one electron at a time, the same wave pattern on the screen.
It did not make sense!
It would mean that confronted to a choice, the electron would lose its particle state, become a wave of potentials, go through both slits and then interfere with itself on the other side!
The other problem with that is that it does not even take into account that the mathematical probabilities still shows the electron could hit the plate and not go through the slate, or that it could still potentially hit just one slit or both. But regardless of the mathematical probabilities, the pattern on the screen is always the same!

Puzzling right? But wait... It becomes even more puzzling and gets to the point of "mind over matter".

Now, puzzled scientists are not happy scientists, so they decided to be sure of what was really, precisely, exactly happening at those slits. So they decided to add detectors/observers at the slits to measure exactly, how many electrons would pass in each and how this all particle/wave nonsense would work.

Now are you ready for this?
The scientists, shot the beam of electrons on to the two slits, ready to measure everything, and guess what? The electrons decided to act like nothing happened and stayed very nicely put as particles, going through the slits,

in orderly manner, hitting the screen with two beautiful parallel lines like the scientists "thought" they should have done originally!!!
The very act of measuring/observing in which slit the electrons would go, meant they did not go through both slits at the same time, but just one as anticipated.

This experiment represents the epitome of what Quantum Physics is to the comprehension of our Universe(s). It opens the doors to many questions about what reality "really" is and how we perceive it.

But, let's go crazy a little, and let's apply this experiment to us as we are made of particles that carry the duality. All that we observe around us including ourselves, through our eyes, is made of particles.
This means that before the observable Universe(s) and ourselves were observed by us, all of it existed as pure waves as well, since we all carry the duality.
But then how could we have observed all of it including ourselves if we did not have a body (i.e. if we were not made of particles, or in other words if we did not have eyes to see, ears to hear, hands to touch, tongues to taste, noses to smell and brains to interpret all these electrical signals)?

It's a catch twenty-two, unless... The simplest answer to this paradox is that what really makes us i.e. our Consciousness must be outside the physical body. Consciousness must exist as the observer. As Consciousness observes, it collapses the world, the Universe(s) into reality.

Our world is in need of quantifying Consciousness. In the same process than Theoretical Physicists want to

find a Theory of Everything that unifies both General Relativity and Quantum Mechanics, researchers on Consciousness might very well be doing the same thing by trying to qualify and quantify Consciousness.
In the String Theory, physicists have mathematically identified nine dimensions. If we look at Consciousness it's easy to identify at least seven.

Each of our senses makes up for one dimension. When we "see" we have a partially accurate notion of our reality, only in one-dimensional sense. Add to that hearing. Now we can identify our reality in two dimensions.

Go on adding all our senses, including the 6th sense (intuition) and a 7th sense (knowing – without learning). The seven known dimensions that our Consciousness contains and brings forward create our reality.

Are there two more dimensions that our Consciousness creates that we haven't discovered yet?

Most likely.

It seems extremely logical to compare Consciousness with the "string" in the String theory that contains all states of the quantum world.
Each state being a sensory perception and the whole being reality as our Consciousness creates it.

Consciousness can thus determine the future of its own reality by choosing to observe or not. In other words, the power of psychokinesis is real. The trouble is our brain might reduce Consciousness ability to truly "see" and "act" upon our Universe(s), by filtering too much of its power.

We can still create harmony and beauty through the filter of our brain but it might require much longer efforts to achieve, which is why we have our entire life to create LOVE and HARMONY.

CHAPTER 8

Déjà vu?

During my senior high school years, still focused on becoming an astrophysicist, I enrolled in an astronomy club about eight miles away from home.

The club was a small club, ran by the President of the Paris Observatory. Our reunions would take place every Tuesday in a small room on the ground of the LRBA (**Laboratoire de recherches balistiques et aérodynamiques** = Ballistic and aerodynamic research laboratory).
All around was military ground and it was also the construction site of the 3rd stage cryogenic engines of Ariane, the European rocket. The place was fantastic! When I was a child, the European space program was working on creating a rocket that would be able to take huge payloads to space.
Ariane 1 blasted into space for the first time from Kourou, French Guiana in 1980. But for years before that they would constantly work on perfecting the rocket and the cryogenic engines were made right at our doorstep. I remember the first time they tried the boosters, our

house was eight miles away and all our windows started to shake. When my dad told me what it was, I was so excited. A rocket being built so close to me, it was unbelievable.
Then it became a game. My dad had explained to me that the boosters had to burn for a certain time to pass the test, so each time they were doing a test, my dad and I would count the number of seconds it lasted and would burst into joy when it would last longer than the previous test - we were keeping tracks.

So every Tuesday evening, my dad and I would go to the astronomy club.
Everyone was very friendly and we had people from all areas. But I was the only girl and apart from a classmate who became later a very prominent researcher and physicist, everyone else was adult!

The evenings would always be divided in two parts. The first hour or so, someone who had been given the task of preparing an exposé on a certain subject, would talk about it. We would share ideas and debate. For the next part, my favorite part, we would take our cars and go deep in military ground and deep in the forest where, thanks to our president, the club had received a substantial amount of money as donations and the men of our club, including my dad, had built a small observatory in which sat like on a throne an amazing Celestron 11 telescope that the subventions had allowed the club to buy.

This was just pure bliss. Even in winter, our fingers were frozen, but there was no way I could miss this. To put my eye on that lens and "see" celestial objects that were so far from us and yet so part of our Universe(s) was indescribable. The feeling of being part of this would every time fill me with tremendous peace and excitement at the same time.

One night, my dad and I were leaving the place after one good night of observation and I was talking casually, making conversation, recalling what we had just observed.
We were walking on the parking lot like we had done a million times before but each time with a different scenario of course. That night, I remember vividly being stopped in my tracks, almost like if a physical hand had been placed on my chest and pushed me so that I would stop walking.

For a few seconds I was disoriented and my dad was looking at me. "What's wrong" he said, "Are you ok?" And I looked at him saying, yes, but "didn't we just walk on this parking lot, like a few seconds ago?"
"What do you mean?" he said.
I repeated myself. I said "Dad, I feel like time stopped and I rewound and replayed what we just did!"
I know what we did is insignificant, but that very specific moment was different. It stopped me; it literally put a halt in my brain.

I know I walked on this parking lot every Tuesday, but this was different. This was like I had a glimpse into another reality.

My dad quickly dismissed the incident but I researched and came to understand I had just had my first powerful "Déjà vu".

Later in my life, I had more of those, but I can honestly

say this one had the most powerful physical effect on me. It stopped me, as I was walking, it put me in a daze for a few long seconds.

Scientific research tends to believe that Déjà vu is a phenomenon due to a memory lapse, an anomaly in which a situation is being recalled in the memory before the brain has had time to process the situation. Without denying the scientific explanation, I think we could also look into the quantum world. Deep down in the quantum world, everything is probability and possibility. It would make sense that a probable or possible situation had interfered with another one, the two possibilities colliding with each other.

By doing so the brain has trouble identifying in which probable or possible situation it belongs to, hence the recall of one situation while living another one.

Again, the Quantum world is offering a rational possibility of explanation to a phenomenon that otherwise would be regarded as a mere "glitch" in our brain.

Scientifically both explanations are equally valid. But I tend to prefer the Quantum rationale, placing our Consciousness at the forefront of the creation of two parallel realities, simultaneously.

CHAPTER 9

"Pape" (Grandpa) on the streets of Istanbul

After the Baccalaureate (the equivalent French exam of the American graduation, crowning the High school years), I was accepted in college to study for two years mathematics and physics in a special program called Math Sup and Math Spe (Mathematics Superior and Mathematics Special equivalent of pretty much four years of college in two). It is pretty much math and physics boot camp.

In France, students call those two years, "La taupe"; translate "The mole" because you are not supposed to see the light of day for two years, studying so hard, locked in your room!

But the Universe(s) had other plans in stock for me.

My wish to become an astrophysicist got cut short by a math professor in Math Sup, who did not allow me to pass in Math Spe. My level in math had become too weak whereas my love for physics was still very much intact.

Because math and physics go hand in hand down the road, the dream was over.

I was so devastated to say the least. I was lost. The only thing I had been thinking about since I was a little child was to study to become an astrophysicist and it all came to an end, crashing with no possible return. (You cannot try again for Math Sup, either you pass, or you are out forever).

My sister who had silently watched my dismay came to my rescue.
"You have a good level in English" she said "You are very talkative and very social, you have a thirst for discovering things and learning and a love for sharing, you should be in Tourism".

Really?

When I failed to integrate Math Spe, my life had taken a spin down because I had been so convinced and so sure of my path since I was a child that the reality had the hardest time to sink in. I was lost for many months.
I was disappointed at myself; I was devastated to have disappointed my dad.
Depression set in.

Hadn't it been for my sister literally fishing me out of the dark waters I was swimming in, I do not know what would have become of me.

It took some convincing on her part with my parents for them to let me change my curriculum to Tourism, and frankly I was not convinced myself either.

I just followed reluctantly, because I had no other options, I was lost and incapable of any decisions anyway.

The two years I spent studying hospitality felt like two years of vacation compared to the rhythm and level of work I had been used to in Math Sup.
I really felt like I was "stupid" as all my life, I had been told by my dad that Math was the only path to success. And look at me now! I was studying tourism, "a complete useless major that would lead me nowhere. " I had been brainwashed letting myself being convinced of the integrity of that statement from my Dad.

So I did not pay much attention during those two years and was more interested in preparing the school festival and show with the student council than really studying.

At the end of those two years one of the students from an anterior promotion, called me to offer me my first job in a tour operator as a sales person. He had become the sales director of that tour operator and he too said, "you have some abilities in talking to people, I know you will be a good sales person."

So I took the job at minimum wage.

But before I started that job, I had to be faced again with death. This time my other grand father, my paternal grand father with whom I was sharing an infinite connection passed away.
This is the man who taught me plants, and gardening. He was so connected with nature. He was also an artist.

He had never learned but was an excellent watercolor painter. I remember his little paintings were all over his bedroom walls. But above all, he was a violinist and a musician. He had taught me how to play piano when I was a child. I remember being allowed to sit at his piano chair or on his laps and looking at his fingers deformed by arthritis playing the scales on the keyboard. But the love of his life was violin. He played violin every day until he had to go to the hospital.

I was 20. He went in for a simple intestine hernia and for whatever reasons, which I will not get into in this book, never really recovered from the operation. He stayed in the hospital for a few months before he passed away. His health gradually deteriorated to the point that we had to feed him, and he was barely cognitive.

One day, I told my dad that my grandpa must have been feeling so sad and so lonely at the hospital without his garden and his violin. I had just received as a gift for my birthday a tape of the Four Seasons by Vivaldi played by a famous symphonic orchestra. The Four Seasons was my grandfather's favorite. So I said to my dad that I wanted my grand father to have my Walkman and I wanted him to listen to Vivaldi because I knew this would soothe him.

On my next visit to the hospital, I brought my Walkman and placed it on my grandpa's head and I started to play the tape. He smiled.

I knew I had gotten through to him.

He died shortly after that. I was devastated.

That night, when the phone rung at my parents' house around 10:00 pm, we all knew who was on the other side of the line. It was not often that you received phone calls that late, back then. My parents left for the hospital after telling my grandma who lived in the other house on the same land.
They told me to stay with my grandma to keep her company and comfort her.

Again, like ten years earlier, the same scenario happened. I was not allowed to go see my grand pa.

So I stayed with her in this big house filled with silence and heaviness.
I comforted her as much as I could. We wept together, hugging and holding hands.

She went to bed after a while and I was to sleep downstairs in the living room where my grand father was playing his violin.
I lied down on the coach there and started to cry. I closed my eyes and after a while of crying, when I had let go of the initial pain and anger, I opened my eyes and there he was, right in front of me. But I could only distinguish his head right behind his musical stand. It was him, there was no doubt. I was not sleeping, I was not dreaming.

It would be today, I would strike a conversation with him, and I would have so many things to ask him. But I was twenty and even though the subject of ESP and life after death fascinated me, to have a direct contact with my grand father's energy was too overwhelming and I left the house running away back to my parents' house. I never told them or my grandma what had happened. My grand father had come back right next to his music stand as if to say "Thank you for the music".

As life went on, I had settled in my new job, though I was a bit of a rookie in the corporate life. I was working hard and enjoying my Parisian life but also taking advantage of what my company had to offer.

A Turkish man owned the company and of course the specialty of this tour operator was to offer products and tours in Turkey (among other European destinations). They even had a charter flight department and each Friday when there were unsold packages to Istanbul, they were offering them to the employees.
I was young and loved to travel and was taking every single opportunity I could to go to Istanbul.

Istanbul is a fascinating city, full of vibrant colors, sounds and smells. I fell in love the first time with its charms, its oddities and its mysteries. There was always also a slight sense of controlled danger to go there by myself but I loved the adrenaline that came with the adventure.

So I was in Istanbul almost every other weekend. My dad had given me his old but very nice Canon camera for my 18th birthday so I had it with me for all my trips.

One of my favorite things to do was to walk from Laleli district where most of our contracted hotels were to the

Kapali Çarsı (Grand Bazaar) stopping at the Istanbul Üniversitesi and the book market on my way. I was taking many pictures and loved to visit and get lost in streets where I would stumble upon beautiful little mosques here and there.

One day, on my daily walk, I came across a very small cemetery. The cemeteries in Turkey are beautiful. Each stone is very high and narrow. The top of the stones is ornamented with turbans for men and other sculptures for women.
It was just beautiful and I started snapping pictures. After a few moments instead of my usual route, I decided for no apparent reason to take the little street to the right of the cemetery, which presented really no special interest, other than another occasion for me to get lost and find little treasures. As I walked I must have snapped a few pictures in that street, but I don't recall anything specific.

When I came back to France, I visited my parents as I usually did on weekends and got my rolls of films developed at the store.
My sister was here and my third degree cousin too, I remember. I opened my photo packets on the dining table, nonchalantly talking about my last trip with my sister and cousin. Then we started to look at the pictures and I was describing to them what was on them and where it was. As I flip one photo, my sister, my cousin and I gasped at the same time and let go of a loud "That's Papé!!!!" (we called our grandpa, Papé)

Right there in the middle of that insignificant little street I had decided to get lost into was a man, totally

centered in my picture, wearing an occidental suit like my grand father had, same color, same cut. The man's demeanor was that of my grandfather. The face was totally blurry but the hair was completely and totally that of my grand father. It was so flagrant that all three of us saw it at the same time without asking each other. And what was more astonishing is that if it was so flagrant in the photo and that man was so in the center of that photo, how come I have no recollection taking that photo purposely?
I believe this was my grand father's way of saying "We are still connected, where ever you go, what ever you do, I am with you and I can be reached".

It clearly indicated that space and time when you are crossed over are not an issue whatsoever!

There is no coincidence. I had to be there that day. It had to happen that way, for me to expand my Consciousness so that the signals of all energies around could flow freely through my right brain.

CHAPTER 10

Full body apparition

Full body apparition is a term that generates many types of reactions. There are the cynical skeptics who will laugh at it, saying it's impossible, it's hallucination or if it's on a film, it is an optical effect; there are the healthy skeptics who will try to find rational reasons but will admit they have no explanations when all known avenues have been explored and there are the "believers" who will think that a full body apparition must be the manifestation of a malevolent spirit trying to hurt you.

TV has contributed to democratize the whole concept of ESP and spirit manifestation. The problem is that it has been sensationalized in the process, killing in the egg the efforts of scientist and healthy skeptics around the world to make sense of it all.

A full body apparition as its term states is when you are confronted with an image of a deceased person appearing before your eyes or on camera. The apparition can be partial or whole, it can be solid or see through.

It can be visible with your own eyes or with Infra Red and Ultra Violet special cameras.

No matter the means, the results are always extremely mind blowing because our left brain cannot rationalize the concept.

Let's go back to the Quantum world for a minute again. In the quantum world all probabilities and all possibilities exist. The Universe(s) as we know it is in fact a superposition of probabilities all happening regardless of time.
A person is alive at a specific place is one reality, a person is dead at the same specific place is another reality. In our three-dimensional world, time becomes a constraint and one reality has to "follow" another or "precede" another.
But in the quantum world both realities in fact exist at the same time.

The Universe(s) is made of information. Imagine the Universe(s) as a gigantic, infinite hard drive where all information of everything is stored. All information exists in that space, but you need a processor to retrieve it.

With a regular computer the processor is key to retrieve that information and bring it to you.
The processor can bring onto your screen a picture of a live person and a picture of that same person deceased, at the same time, as long as it is stored on the hard drive.

For the Universe(s) it is the same. Quantumly all information is stored in the Universe(s) in the form of probabilities and possibilities.
We, the processors bring forward the stored information. The problem is that we human have a very limited processor, the brain, which seems to have trouble bringing several probabilities at the same time upfront.

As observers of the Universe(s) most of us, humans, collapse into one reality at a time.

Does that mean there is only one reality? Absolutely not! It just means we have a hard time processing more than one at the same time!

What if we were given once in a while the possibility to get a glimpse at processing two realities at the same time? One of the infinite realities where your loved one is alive and one of the infinite realities where your loved one is dead?

What if seeing an apparition was just that, an incursion in the quantum world?
It would most definitely result in full body apparitions.

It seems to me very plausible.

CHAPTER 11

The awakening

At Age 17 I had worked all summer to pay for my first trip to the US and my parents let me go and stay with an American family for one month.
The connection I had felt when I was a child with the US had been finally revealed to me and I felt home when I arrived.
I had a great time and fell in love for the first time with a young American college student.

Our long distance relationship lasted on and off until my early twenties and had failed to rekindle on his last visit to Paris when I realized our goals and ways of life were different.

So I forgot about him.

By then, I had been living the life of a young college student in Paris, studying hard and partying harder. But with my minimum wage work came a time of reality check and I was not very happy at my job.

One day, after a couple of years of hiatus in ESP, and years after my last contact with my American boyfriend, I woke up in my one room apartment in Paris, with one repetitive sentence in my mind: "John* is going to give me some news, John is going to give me some new!"
* name was changed to preserve privacy.

I could not shake that thought off my mind, all morning. When I finally ran down the three stories from my apartment down to the street to go catch the next subway to my work (I was not an early bird…), I automatically opened my mailbox as I would do every day, and there it was, a letter from John. And it hit me like a ton of bricks.
The whole time I knew it was coming, the whole time I knew I was going to get some news.

That moment was the starting point of my reconvening with my right brain and getting reacquainted with my ESP.

And it started to pick up from that point with little things here and there, getting gradually to bigger things and negative things. I was starting to feel the pain and disarray of people who were total strangers to me.

The first big event that got me all shook up happened in the Parisian subway.

I was going to work, business as usual and waiting for the next train to arrive at the station. People started to agglomerate in front of me in expectation of the train. I was always staying back for fear of a crazy person pushing.

The train finally arrived and came to a stop. The crowd had already rushed to the doors waiting for them to open. And as I started to walk towards one set of doors, I stopped in my tracks. My legs started to hurt terribly. I thought they were on fire. I remember dropping my briefcase and holding my shins with both my hands wondering what was going on with me.

In the few seconds it took me to experience these sensations, I heard a scream and people started yelling to make sure the train conductor would not close the doors and go.
An older lady had missed the step to get in the train and had fallen her two legs down between the train step and the edge of the platform and was stuck there. The emergency signal went off and they retrieved the lady who had both the shins of her legs severely scratched and wounded.
It was such a strange feeling when I realized my pain was linked to the lady's pain.
I started thinking, what is the point of me feeling this if I cannot change the outcome?

It really started to work its way to my soul and clearly opened up a new window of personal research.

Fast forward to a Friday of September 1989.
I was working as a sales representative in a Tour Operator in Paris. I was twenty-one.

The office was located in a small building right in the heart of the 9th district of Paris, close to La Madeleine church and a few blocks away from the Concorde Square, at the bottom of the Champs Elysees Avenue; infamous square where the French Revolution saw its worst atrocities with the guillotine of thousands of people.

The city's last great architectural development before modern time happened during the Haussmann period in the 1860's. Baron Haussmann's civic planning of the city had started to rebuild a new clean Paris. He was at the time highly criticized for its extravagance but in fact gave Paris its famous look of long sleek avenues, with beautiful organized buildings that we see today. Most buildings built during that period are about four to five story high and have a courtyard. Today they harbor a mix of residential apartments and offices.

That Friday of September 1989, I was on my lunch break. With my colleagues we had just come back up from having lunch in our usual cafe downstairs.
We had gathered in the small entrance hall of our office and we were chatting in front of the window.

From that window we could see the inside of the courtyard. We were on the third floor. It was not uncommon to see other people walking by their windows inside their own apartments or offices on the other side of the courtyard. That day, though, as we were chatting, my eyes caught a gentleman wearing black slacks and a white shirt, like a business attire, walking by one of the windows on the 5th floor.

I saw him for about two seconds, the time it took him to walk from one side of the window to the other side where he disappeared from my view in his office. But I froze.

All of the sudden, in a trance like attitude, I went from having a mundane conversation with girl colleagues to totally, involuntarily say: "Don't jump! Why would you want to jump, don't jump, please!" and then I snapped out of my trance like state and looked around me like I had been gone for a while.

It was the weirdest thing that had ever happened to me.

My colleagues were looking at me with this big question mark hovering above their head.
Then they started to ask me questions: "why did you say that?"
I had no clue.
"I don't know, I don't know!!!" I said; feeling very confused.
All windows were closed, we could not hear anything from the outside and vice versa.
We brushed off the incident and went back to work. At around four in the afternoon, I was at my desk. I was working when the loudest "BAM!" noise startled all of us.

Instantly, I started shaking. My entire body was shaking uncontrollably. I said at loud: "Oh my God, He jumped!"
My boss looked at me with this puzzled stare: "What are you talking about?"

I kept repeating, "He jumped; he jumped!"

I knew, deep inside my soul, that he had jumped.

I was crying. I was frantic. People in the office were looking at me like if I was crazy.
I stood up and I was really scared to go look at the window. Everybody went to look. They opened the windows overlooking the courtyard and people started screaming.

My worst fear had come true.

The gentleman indeed had jumped, from the 5th floor to his death.

The paramedics arrived very fast, tried everything they could to revive him for about forty minutes or so, it seemed a very long time, and then from my vantage point I saw one of them waving his hand in a "stop everything" manner. It was over.

They placed him in a black body bag. I remember them putting his shoes on top.
They took him away.

I had to be dismissed that day because I was a wreck. I remember taking the subway to go back to my studio, picking up my travel bag and driving to go see my parents in the countryside for the weekend. I remember seeing the sun setting on the highway and thinking how life was so precious and wondering WHY, WHY, WHY couldn't have I done anything to prevent that, since I had felt it so strong, without even knowing this person... I was so confused. I was so angry with him and with myself.

THIS was the turning point in my quest to understand Consciousness and its connections with life, death and us all.
That year, a series of events of that sort happened to me and I knew I really had to find my path in order to help people.

I had to find a purpose in all this.

>That event specifically was the catalyst for my endeavor to unravel the truth and ramifications of Consciousness and how we can communicate with it when it is remote.

CHAPTER 12

Connecting with Consciousness: A child's aptitude we should encourage

Medical science shows that we clearly have "two distinct brains". To simplify to the extreme, we will call them the left brain and the right brain.

Our left brain is the one that helps you read this book, the one that makes you get up every day and go to work, balance your check book, plan for your future, calculate the distance between one city to another, organize your life and most of all, rationalize the information received every second from your environment.
Our left brain has that capacity to receive information from outside stimuli and tries to find something it knows already to quickly identify and process the information using association.
That same left brain is the one that will not let you sleep at night, because it can't stop "thinking". That left brain can become an annoyance if you let it take over.

Our right brain on the contrary is the one that allows you to appreciate music, to feel the beauty of nature, to love your child, without asking questions, without trying to rationalize the reasons why. Our right brain lets in much more information from outside stimuli because it has no need to make sense of it; it just lets it happen. And by doing so it creates a bridge with the Universe(s), a bridge where the information can cross from the quantum level to our dimension with almost no restriction.

As Dr Melvin Morse, pioneer in NDE and Consciousness research and bestseller author of "Closer to the light" puts it in his new book "Falsely accused, a spiritual journey",
"In neuro-scientific terms, our ego (the little brain) represents the left brain's take on reality, which it creates with a mere 10,000 bits of information per second. In order to restructure our spiritual take on life, we have to reach back into our spiritual "right brain" Consciousness (the six billion bits of information per second directly linked to the informational Universe(s)'s mainframe) and pull out a different 10,000 bits of information. We then use this new information to create a new shared local reality with different and improved spiritual values."

When we "tap" into information such as feeling someone's distress and will to end his own life without knowing the person, we in fact tap into the informational Universe(s) and let our right brain soak in it.
Because our right brain has been proven to carry a major role in processing our emotions, it shows that we become aware of that new information by triggering our emotional reaction to it. (C.K. Mills was one of the

first researchers to propose a direct link between th
right hemisphere and emotional processing which
to the creation of the Right Hemisphere Hypothesis or
Valence Hypothesis).

It is why most psychic mediums in the field will talk
about "feeling" the connection with the deceased
person, or the person incapacitated like in a coma. "It's
making me feel like…." is a common saying among us.
All perceptions we get are either visual, auditory or
olfactory; or all of them. But they all trigger emotions,
they all trigger sensations that pass through our brain
and body like a ripple effect after a rock has been
tossed in water.
The key in mediumship is to let the right brain take
over and to tone down the left brain.
Our left brain wants to explain, wants to rationalize
and make sense of what it perceives because that's how
we survive. As a species, we need that capacity to
recognize dangers and to thrive against adversity, we
need to learn and acquire knowledge to stay alive in
our bodies.

What is a psychic medium? Nothing special, really.
Because we, humans, are all psychic. We all have the
capacity to tap into our informational Universe(s) and
retrieve information. It's the way we process it that
makes some people more "psychic" than others.

We are all born psychics. It is not uncommon to hear
stories about young children reporting seeing deceased
loved ones who have been long gone before they were
even born. Children "know" how to connect because

their brain has not been polluted yet by "left brain knowledge". Children have no preconceived ideas on how things work and thus are much more open and much more inclined to let their right brain pick up all kinds of sensory perceptions and not try to analyze them.

Every parent on Earth, at one point or another, has had to deal with the inevitable questions from their children: "What do you mean Grandma is dead?" "Where is heaven?" "Why can't I see it?" "Are "ghosts" real?" "What is God?" As those taunting questions are not as embarrassing as "How are babies made?" they are nevertheless extremely difficult to answer without getting ourselves all entangled with our own fears and questions about the subject.

Children have the deepest insights on most things in life. Before they are taught not to believe, not to love, no to listen to their "heart" or to their "inside voice", they are the most armed human beings against any prejudice and any preconceived ideas about everything really.

But this statement is especially true for what children perceive Consciousness is. They actually don't perceive it. They intrinsically know with no judgment or fear until they are taught the contrary.

They know how to listen with their heart, they know how to trust their right brain; they know how things work. They are attuned to Consciousness frequency and they can tap into it far better than any psychic could do after years of intensive training.

The key in helping our children to keep their openness is to go with the flow, to not dismiss any "weird" or "strange" affirmations they can make sometimes. But to go along with those affirmations, and help them investigate their own potential.

There are countless examples of children reporting seeing and talking to a dead relative they did not even know, who even passed before they were born. And yet they recognize their connection as real and palpable and tangible and meaningful. It is so real to them that dismissing it would be dismissing your child's own mental sanity.
I am not saying that all accounts of talking to an "imaginary friend or relative" have to be considered as true facts. But when those accounts can clearly be backed up with factual evidence such as the description, name and general behavior of the deceased the child supposedly connected with, matching those of a real family member crossed over, one parent has the responsibility to gently pursue the matter and not dismiss it as fabrication.
In turn it will help the child keep his heart and Consciousness open to the flow of information that is right here, everywhere, all the time, ready to be accessed.

Fast-forward a few years. My own daughter surprised me when her deep connection with Consciousness was revealed to me one morning.
At the tender age of eighteen months my daughter was a lovely, very cute, very bubbly girl, who was exuding joy and loving energy. But she was yet to speak her first words.

All she had was one word. This word was not even a word that existed in the three languages we are speaking at home and that we were teaching her, being a multicultural family: French, English and Spanish. Each time we would go outside, she would point at the moon and would say "tam". Only my husband and I would know what "tam" meant in her own one word vocabulary. Tam meant moon. Moon in French is lune and in Spanish is luna... Not even close to "tam". But tam was her word for moon and it was also her only word. It would worry me a lot that she would not speak any other words, not even mom, mommy or daddy, or dad.
I became so worried, because one of my nieces had been diagnosed with Asperger syndrome years earlier, that I convinced my husband to have our daughter tested.

I remember sitting there in this tiny room with the child therapist who was a very sweet lady. The therapist proceeded to tell us they would not test her with the regular test for her age, because it required understanding and use of language, which she did not have.
So they used a different type of testing which covered five different areas of development (1) Using hands and body – 2) Eating, dressing and Toileting – 3) Expressing and Responding to feelings and interacting with others – 4) Playing, thinking, exploring and 5) Understanding and communicating.

I was very anxious but my daughter "performed" pretty well that day and when the results came back, it was very interesting to say the least.

Number 2, 4 and 5 tests, with number 5 test getting the lowest result off all, were all three on the very lower limit of the typical range for a child her age. No real surprise there but she was still in the range, even though she was at the lower limit.
Number 1 was completely in the middle of the range coinciding with total normal average for her age.

But what was astonishing was number 3. Her ability to "express and respond to feelings and to interact with others" was way above the upper limit of typical range for her age!

So we went, reassured that she would eventually talk one day. (We were even told that once she would start, she would probably never stop and… Well the prophecy came true! She is a nonstop talker. She hasn't been awake for more than two seconds, and this is with no exaggeration, that she starts talking, and talking, and talking and never stops until she finally falls into a deep sleep at night!). So much for worrying!

Back when she was little, my daughter had her little routine. She would wake up around 7:00 am, I would bring her a bottle of milk and I would lie there on the floor of her bedroom while she was drinking and then playing. I would use this time to just rest and fully wake up gradually.

I am also a woman of routines!
I always have breakfast with a large cup of Earl Grey tea. I cannot start my day without that.

One morning, my daughter woke up as usual, I brought her milk to her as usual, and as I laid down on the floor of her bedroom, particularly tired and unable to shake sleep off, I started to think to myself that this fatigue could only be tackled by a cup of coffee, and a strong one. A cup of tea like I usually did would not cut it. And I started to think: "hum, I am going to get up and make myself a cup of coffee." Very unusual for me and totally out of my early morning routine; coffee on an empty stomach is something I am not found of but for some reason that morning, I was so tired, it became a prominent thought in my mind while I was laying there with my daughter.

And as I was thinking and envisioning the cup of coffee in my head, my "one word" child who hadn't been able to say mom or dad or anything else in the whole wide world since she was born, sat up, looked right at me and boasted a loud: "CAFÉ?!" (Coffee in French).

My child who had not spoken any word ever other than the one invented word for moon, connected with my feelings, totally embraced by Consciousness and made it clear to me that she knew "exactly" what she was talking about and what I was thinking.
Mommy needed a coffee, and excuse me, but in French on top of everything!

I looked at her in disbelief and of course as soon as I tried to rationalize the moment and asked her "what did you just say?" she went back to her playing, totally ignoring my request, like nothing had happened.

My jaw dropped and I knew at that moment, that my baby was totally fine and actually even finer than I expected; she had a right brain developed beyond what I thought.

All of the sudden, the "way above the higher range limit for her age relating to others' feelings" test results came back to me and made total sense. Not only was she able to relate to people's feelings, reading body language and facial expressions, but also she was able to connect, at least with me, on a much deeper and higher level of Consciousness.

It was astounding! She never said the word "café" again until she was able to really speak and had to learn the word in French all over again years later!

Over the course of the last four and a half years since her eighteen month old "Café" episode, my daughter has surprised us many times on similar, coming out of nowhere, expressions, words, questions and affirmations that she could not possibly have heard and yet knew.

Of course, my passion for the matter of Consciousness and the Continuum of it after Death, has lead me to leave the door open for her for any questions she might have. I treat each one of them with an open mind and without pushing the issue or the subject on her. But when she comes with a legitimate question, I don't give her the run around of heaven and angels. I tell her how I see things. I tell her about the LOVE that never dies, I tell her that our Consciousness or spirit or soul, is always around and that when we shed our body, which is a natural thing, we can still continue as pure energy and that it is not impossible to connect and communicate with that energy, as long as we keep the LOVE IN OUR HEART. And she gets it.

My daughter is now six years old at the time I am writing this book. As I am a science-oriented type of person, we also have conversations about nature, Earth and the evolution of things and beings on Earth. I must have told her once that we (including her) were sharing a common ancestor with apes way back, because she came to me the other day and asked me (always out of left field): "Mommy, why can't I remember being an ape?"

I love my daughter's questions because they force me to find the right easy, six year old kind of words, to explain notions that are quite complicated. So here I am trying to recreate the world from the Big Bang to the creations of atoms and gas, then stars and galaxies and planets, and Earth and the apparition of life on Earth, starting with amebae and fish, then reptilians and dinosaurs, onto mammals and apes and, here we are primitive humans all the way to modern time humans… I want to talk about all this to get to my point for her, which is "if our Consciousness, our soul had to remember all this, it would be way too much for our brain and we would not be able to process all the information! And I proceed to tell her, look how difficult it is already to remember your multiplication tables! Imagine if you had to remember all the times and lives you've had!!! Too much stuff!

(The adult explanation would be that our Consciousness lives simultaneously all these episodes on Earth due to its Quantum field of possibilities, and not in a linear manner, but all at once. So in fact those different realities are not interfering with each other, though sometimes they do, and that's when we think we "remember" when in fact we are given a tiny opening in the window of other life probabilities... but that would be a little too much for a six year old...)

So as I am trying to make my point, she stops me and says: "But, who created Earth?"

Ah ah ... OK... so to me our Universe(s) exists only because Consciousness exists and can collapse realities by observing them... Again, a bit too out there for a six year old... so I just go and say: "Well some people call it God, I call it Consciousness".
So she stops and ponders for a moment and then bolstering a huge smile and a sparky look in her eyes, that says "oh I got it", she goes "Oh ok, that's easy then, its first name is God and its last name is Consciousness!"

And that's how God Consciousness created the world!

Children are so much more intuitive than we become as adult. They intuit the right path, the highest level of profound philosophical ideas.

I had always had a problem with the word God, because it is always associated with religion and I am an atheist. But I knew that LOVE and CONSCIOUSNESS were the keys to our Universe(s). When my daughter made it so simple for me, I realized, it was OK to use the word God, because, it really is a first name, and Consciousness a last name. The two names are indivisible, they are ONE; they are two faces of the same coin. That coin is what I call the "I-ther" of the Universe(s). Call it the Theory of Everything, or anything Science has been trying to discover, God Consciousness is the I, ME, and the infinite collection of MEs that weave the very fabric of the Universe(s) at the astronomical level and at the quantum level.

My six-year-old daughter intuited that!

The new term my six year old daughter had coined made so much sense that Dr. Melvin Morse used it in his new book "wrongfully accused, a spiritual journey" after I shared the anecdote with him. He used it to define the Information Field where all that makes the Universe(s) is encompassed.

"I believe the children are our future
Teach them well and let them lead the way
Show them all the beauty they possess inside
Give them a sense of pride to make it easier
Let the children's laughter remind us how we used to be"

I believe the lyrics of this beautiful song, interpreted by Whitney Houston, clearly demonstrate that we need to let our children explore the vastness of their own Consciousness while guiding them and grounding them with LOVE, KNOWLEDGE and mutual RESPECT. We as parents should encourage them to use their right brain, to keep the connection with the informational Universe(s) flowing.
    Because we are all psychic, we are ONE with the Universe(s).

CHAPTER 13

On my way to a career path

Back to my life in Paris, way before I had children. After my overwhelming experience with the man who committed suicide, I felt a push and my childhood curiosity and passion came back full force.
Two things pushed me.
One was my American ex boy friend who had made amend and was coming back to my life and the other my wish to be successful enough to have time and money. I was young!

I started to make plans to move to the US. I sent out spontaneous resumes to American tour operators, many of them. I had no experience what so ever or so very little, I had no chance.

In the midst of all this, very quickly my American boyfriend and I came to a definite halt in our relationship. Too many differences.
But I had the will.

When the resumes I sent to the US failed to produce job offers, I sought another job in France. I sent out a

resume to another French company and got hired by this man who became my mentor. He was the owner of a small tour operator.
But his specialty was Asia; he was not producing any trips to the US.

He hired me as a sales person again. After a while, I went to see him and told him I was bored. I entered into a demonstration to show him that he was missing a lot of business by not producing on the US market. I told him I could help him create such a market for him. And against all odds he told me: " Fine, build me a department, make it successful and I will back you up to create your own company in the US, you have carte blanche".

I was twenty-three!

I was on cloud nine!

He taught me the basics of everything and after many trips together to the US to negotiate prices, inspect sites and create itineraries, our department became so successful that he decided we should push it a notch.

He had me move and share business and office with an established receptive operator specialized on Mexico, thinking he could share the huge clientele of this operator.

I worked really hard because I wanted to make this successful to eventually move to the US.

After three years of working hard and waiting, nothing

happened. No offer to back me up came, and sadly I had to say goodbye to my mentor. He had played his very important role but did not fulfill his promise.

I was hired by a company, which represented a group of receptive operators around the world. The company had started to integrate and create their own offices in each country but for the biggest market, the US they were still representing external companies in which they did not have any shares.

This was going to be my biggest opportunity yet to achieve my goal and I totally threw myself in it.

But again, life had other plans for me in store, because I needed to learn a couple of more things before I could attain the dream.

I had met this man who had decided to create his own receptive operator in South Africa. The country was leaning towards the end of the Apartheid and much was to be done there. The market was extremely promising.
Pushed by blind love and a new possible business opportunity I derailed from my path.

I successfully convinced my new employees to create with me a company specialized in the South African destination, which would allow me to mix business and my newfound love.

Within a year the company became very successful considering the novelty market it was developing and the owners of the mother company finally approached me and asked me if I would be interested in helping them create their receptive operator in the US.

As it coincided precisely with the biggest love deception of my life, I did not even think twice. At last one of my dreams was coming through!

I sold my shares in my company and moved on!

During all these years my focus had turned to building a career, being successful, attaining a dream. It was also to conjure my failure in continuing my studies in math and physics and to prove to my parents and myself that I could still be happy doing something else.

But immigrating to the US was much more than that. It was like coming back home. I was in much need of a new life, a clean slate for my soul and my heart, which both had been used and abused badly during the preceding year.

The incredible connection I felt while establishing in Sausalito, CA, was beyond liking a country.
I remember, each time I was crossing the Golden Gate Bridge, coming back from a business trip to France, my heart would rejoice. I remember smelling the eucalyptus trees and thinking, "I am home at last."
The connection was visceral.
I felt a keen with the American people more than I felt one with my own country.

The attraction I felt as a child for the West was coming back to me full force and this time with a purpose.

I had sort of put on the back burner my soul searching about ESP and life after death in the race to become someone and being respected in the professional world.

And now, I could feel my heart reopening to the Universal energy, feeling connected again, and ready to continue the search.

CHAPTER 14

Visiting another life

One day, I was coming back from a trip to France, and I was sitting on the plane drifting away listening to meditation music from one of the channels of the inflight entertainment. It was a long flight. Eleven hours, non-stop to Oakland, CA from Paris. I was not sleeping but I was totally at peace, relaxed and not thinking. The perfect altered state of Consciousness I would learn later for connecting with signal lines of energies around us.

I was not thinking of anything, I was just one with the present moment. It was a wonderful feeling.

While I was enjoying drifting to this beautiful altered state of Consciousness, like a dream sneaking up on me, a very vivid and clear image of an old western town appeared to me. I could see a building on the right, and I knew instantly it was a hotel.

Then like a movie director, I could see the entire scene. I was looking at a slice of time.

The odd part was that there was a lady in front of me, turning her back to me, walking on the main street of that western town. Her beautiful Victorian light blue dress was making her tiny waist looking even smaller. Her hair arranged in an elaborate bun was brown and clearly well taken care of. She was exuding confidence and at the same time sadness. All of this took a split second to happen in my mind but I knew also instantly I was her.
The odd thing though was that I was detached from her, I was looking at her. It was the strangest feeling. I knew that she was the owner of the building to the right.
The street was sandy and dusty. There was no one there except her.
To her left there were three trees that created a little centerpiece in the town, like a town square. I knew those trees were oaks. As all this information came to my mind, I also realized my name was Mary and we were in 1882.

Next thing I knew, I saw a man down the street and in the blink of an eye, three other men were on him and he fell to the floor, he had just been shot.
I knew, again in an instant, that this man on the floor was my husband; I knew simultaneously he was the Sheriff of the town and I knew he was shot dead by those three men.

Without any transition I found myself on top of a hill. Once again, I knew it was me, but I was looking at me from behind, still. I still hadn't seen my face.
And in an instant again, I knew I was pregnant even though I could only see myself from the back.

I was pointing a gun at my temple and then without hesitation, I pulled the trigger and killed myself.

Then again, without any form of transition, I saw myself, on a Native American burial sepulture or scaffold, with Native American people whom I felt I knew as family, dancing around.

And then, I came back from my trance. As I sat there on the plane's seat, I was in total shock. I was stunned. I did not know what to think of all this. I know I was not sleeping. This was not a dream. This was different. It felt so real, so intense and yet so puzzling because I was missing so many pieces of the puzzle to fully understand what had happened.
I tried to brush it off but it stuck.
It is now been more than twenty years as I am writing this book and I still remember vividly every single detail of that very unique experience.

As I landed, life got back to usual, but I kept thinking about that "dream state" episode and wanted to get answers.
One day, someone said to me "You know, you might as well have had a glimpse into one of your past lives"

It hit me like a ton of bricks! It was the answer; it was obvious! I had somehow put myself in such an altered state of Consciousness that I had been able to access one of my other lives. And then everything became clear.

My attraction for the US and the West and my uncanny love for Native Americans since I was a little child in

France (for no apparent reason), my transition from trying to be an astrophysicist to being in tourism and hospitality thanks to my sister, which for many years had no sense for me (I owned a hotel in this past life) and my fear of guns associated with suicide: when I was still living in France, I had befriended a gentleman who was a police officer. But he was also a biker and had a lot of biker friends. Some of them were good and some of them not so good. My boyfriend at the time had invited his brother to stay with us for a few days as he was going through a rough psychological patch and was suicidal, so we could monitor him closely. One night, our police officer friend and us were invited to have dinner at a biker friend's apartment in Paris.

The whole idea was to try to cheer my boyfriend's brother up a little.
I had no idea how it would turn.
As the dinner went on, they made my boyfriend's brother talk to try and help him get everything out. It was pretty intense.
But as my boyfriend's brother kept on saying negative things about himself, I could feel the tension building up in the guys. And all of the sudden, my friend police officer drew his gun and placed it on the table and said: "You really want to kill yourself, heh?" "Then do it now!"
At that moment, a sheer panic attack engulfed me to the point that I was shaking and crying. I kept looking at the gun, I couldn't think. All I could see was this gun and my whole body was shaking, I was not thinking of my boyfriend's brother anymore, I was not seeing anyone in the room, the whole room was spinning and I was in a trance like. The gun, the gun! I remember

starting begging my friend to get the gun away, please get the gun away.
After what felt like hours, it was only a few minutes, my friend police officer got the gun back and opened it to show us it was empty and put it back in his holster under his jacket. The whole incident created a platform of conversation that lasted all night and I believe in a way helped my boyfriend's brother. Call it cop psychology if you want!

But fast forward to my dream like state on the plane to California a few months later and I see me, killing myself with a gun! No wonder I was so upset that night in Paris when my friend taunted my boyfriend's brother to do it with his gun to provoke a reaction.

It all fell into place. The only problem was that I only had fragments of that life and it opened more questions than it gave me answers.

It would take a little over ten years to finally get the missing pieces of the puzzle and being able to close that chapter of my life and make peace with it thanks to a professional hypnotist and friend who would take me through that path again and have me finish the story.

This event was the sparkle that ignited the fire and the thirst for reading books in me. From that moment I started to read every single book I could find on ESP, mediumship, life after death, meditation, death and dying, quantum physics, past life regressions, Consciousness and its nature, NDE, you name it. I became this well that could never get enough water of knowledge to fill it up.

And I started to realize that all my experiences, all those events that paved my journey happened for a reason. And that reason was to open my mind to the possibility, the probability of Consciousness being much more than what we think it is.

The long quest of what I was supposed to do with all these sensory perceptions started to take shape in my mind into something more concrete, more purposeful, something that later would finally redesign my entire life.

That last experience made me realize that the linear notion of time had no meaning, because I was able to see, feel, smell, touch, taste and hear as vividly as when the events occurred in the 1800's.

The question was, was I replaying the events with my soul, my energy or was I able to actually transpose myself as a light being into that space/time location of the Universe(s).

It all made a big circle back to why I was so interested in physics and astrophysics. All my life made sense.

I went on with my career path and jumped from one company to create my very own on the East coast, still managing to be a business oriented woman and a deeply spiritual individual for lack of a better word. (I do not like the word spiritual because it is tainted with religious connotation and I am totally not a religious person.)

I spent more and more time reading, finding what others were thinking or studying in the field of Consciousness and energy.

I started practicing ESP on my friends and family, getting sensory perceptions about their lives and sometimes their loved ones... They started asking me to do readings for them.

One night, I remember sitting on my sofa watching TV when this new show came on. It was "Crossing over with John Edward".
I was fascinated, not by the ability that he was displaying, as I believed we all have it, but by the fact that I had never thought that we could put it to work that way.

The man who met his death, committing suicide jumping from the fifth floor from years before finally had found his purpose in my mind. I could actually use my perception to really help, to really bring comfort, to even change people's lives.
It was an amazing moment.

I still did not know how I would apply that knowledge, but I had a much better direction.
So I continued reading for my friends and families and the friends of my friends.

Soon word of mouth became strong enough that I put a website up.

I was working in two different directions. One was reading for people's lost loved ones and the other was studying intelligent interaction in places that had presented unexplained phenomena such as voices, full bodied apparitions and the like.

I soon came up with my own interpretation of how Consciousness works and how it affects our human senses.

CHAPTER 15

"You can only see if you pay attention!" – NOT!

In the course of my many trips to South Africa, I had somehow succeeded with no intention of doing so to infuse the same interest in my partner and boyfriend for astronomy. Observing the sky had become a nice thing to do at night just the two of us or with friends.

The sky in the southern hemisphere is an absolute spectacle of lights and when the air pollution is not too intense, lying outside looking at its glorious light infused darkness fills you with such joy and happiness. I remember, my very first trip to South Africa. I was so happy to go for many different reasons; but one of them was because I knew I was going to see the south sky for the first time and I was very excited.
In preparation of that event, I remember going to the store "La Maison de l'Astronomie" (The Astronomy House) in Paris to buy sky maps in order to identify what I would come to first see and discover in the sky down there.

After my partner became interested in the matter he bought maps as well.

On one of my trips, one night we decided to go outside in the garden to look at the sky.
If you have never had the chance to see the sky in the southern hemisphere, you have to imagine the celestial vault of the northern hemisphere, by the best night without clouds and pollution, perhaps, sitting on a bench outside a cabin in the mountains, high above the sea level and far from any city lights; and multiply the shimmering beauty that you immerse yourself into by a hundred!

It is better than any multimillion-dollar fireworks, better than any man made show of lights could ever dream to achieve.

Pair it with your favorite music and I guarantee you will fly high!

Now that I knew I had left sort of an imprint in my partner's mind with my love for astronomy, I started to discuss with him about the constellations we could see and my favorites, asking him what his were.

Then I came to say: " I know it's probably lame, but my favorites are the Large Magellanic Cloud (LMC) and the Small Magellan Cloud (SMC)"; I said lame, because they were not some rare constellations or formations in the sky they actually were and are so big and so bright, you cannot miss them.
It's just amazing to know that you are seeing with your own eyes two of the very few closest galaxies to our own Milky Way, without even needing a pair of binoculars!

The night was perfect, the sky was bright and I was just in awe.
Until my partner said: "But I don't see them" " I Have tried but I don't see them!"

It startled me because, anywhere I would look in the vastness of the starry night, my eyes would still catch a glimpse of the two galaxies without even looking for them.

They look like a big white milky like ovoid stain in the sky!

And that my partner would not see them was leaving me in disbelief.
I thought he was joking at first. But when he became dead serious and annoyed at my "What? You can't see them, but that's impossible, they are right here, so huge!" I realized he was not joking.

After dismissing any eye problem as he was seeing very well other stars and constellations we would go over with together, I remained baffled.

The whole situation turned into an argument because to me I could not understand how something so big and beautiful could not be seen and he could not understand why I would not get it!

He finally told me:
"If you don't know it's there, If you don't pay attention, meticulously, you can't see it".

But he knew where they were supposed to be, he had the sky maps, and besides, my point was, even without a sky map, it seemed impossible to miss them.

A few days later, we had travelled to Mozambique to check new hotels and possible tourism development. As we were in our hotel room, watching the Rugby World Cup, some how, the conversation came back to the forefront.

He suddenly grabbed the window drapes that had colorful patterns of different shapes and hues and told me: "close you eyes!"
I had no idea where he was going with that, but I closed my eyes.
Then he proceeded to say: "Now describe the curtains! They've been here all along, but can you describe what's on them? Can you see what's there?"

Well, certainly if I close my eyes it will be a bit more difficult, I suppose you would not try to find the Magellanic clouds your eyes closed but, I made my point very clear:

You don't need to pay attention to see what's there, you need to immerse yourself and let your soul be impregnated by the beauty of what's in front of you.

If I had been given the right settings of a quiet and peaceful discussion, I am sure that I would have been able to describe the curtains, eyes closed, because I would have immersed myself into the reality of the curtains in the room and get all kinds of sensory perceptions of shapes and colors! No doubt about it!

127

But it was not a relaxed conversation. He wanted me to admit I could not describe the curtains.

The problem in his demonstration, is that we were not trying to look at the curtains, neither of us had a passion for the curtains, nor did we spend time starring at the curtains prior to that event... So it kind of defeated his point.

What really happened is that he was not seeing the Magellanic Clouds, not because he was not paying attention, but on the contrary, because he was too meticulous trying to find them based on a sky map in lieu of letting him soak into the beauty of the sky.

Once you "see" with your soul, then it's easy to find it back with a map.

That day I understood even deeper the meaning of seeing with my heart.

When you do not let your left brain interfere with your vision and on the contrary let your right brain be bathed in your environment, you can see much deeper and much clearer than if you try too hard to see.

For my partner, that night, not seeing the Magellanic Clouds was probably a case of trying too hard to see them with maps and calculation and forgetting to abandon himself deep in the beauty of the sky.

A very clear demonstration of how a psychic medium works vs. a non-psychic person. The psychic or psychic trained person will get the information first through meditation then will identify its place into the chart of the sitter's experience.

A non-psychic trained or left brain oriented person, will go after the information and look for the information into an almost infinite number of possibilities of space time realities, failing almost all the time to find it.
It's important to remember than being psychic is given to everyone who allows oneself to open without trying too hard. Learning to let go is probably the most important tool in mediumship and CRV.

The lesson learned from that odd conversations and moments back in South Africa is that you don't have to look to see. And by derivation, you do not have to listen to hear, or touch to feel. It can happen at a much higher level of Consciousness, if you let go.

CHAPTER 16

Past life regression, reincarnation, or is it really in the past?

When we talk about life after death, the door is open to many speculations.

If our Consciousness is not a product of brain activity but in fact exists as a major component of the fabric of the Universe(s), how does it "attach" itself to a body? Why does it do so? And if it can "attach" itself and "detach" itself, can it do it repeatedly? So many questions and no clear answers. Yet, as much as we do not have the answers to these very core questions of our existence, we do have the ability of getting glimpses of their probabilities and possibilities. After all we are ourselves a field of probabilities materialized in one specific possibility among an infinite number of possibilities. The quantum level of us is the best witness of that fact.

Because of how the quantum level of the Universe(s) works, we cannot ignore the fact that there is a valid interrogation about having different materializations of "us".

The question is, are we talking about Consciousness being incarnated in a body in the "past", and while in another body in the "present", having a glimpse of memory of that specific previous life? Or are we talking about Consciousness being collapsed at the quantum level into two or multiple realities (an infinite really) and having some of these realities interfere with one another creating a false memory of a "past life" when indeed those lives, are superimposed, at the same time?

In view of that question, I believe that past lives can be looked at from two different angles.
First, let's look at the hypothesis that Consciousness does reincarnate in a new body after the physical death of another one. This hypothesis suggests a linear time and progression of life, which we are of course very familiar with, as our lives are totally wrapped around time. We wake up every morning, counting a new day. There is today, there was yesterday, and then there will be tomorrow. We completely organize our life around that notion of time that we believe starts in the past, is in the present and continues in the future. It's easy to believe this is how it works, as we observe the Universe(s) changing, evolving, galaxies spinning, and stars being created and dying.

The cycles we observe as humans make us believe that we are indeed prisoners of a time constricted Universe(s) where everything has to have a beginning, even if we can't determine how and when, and everything has to have an end.

We some how condition ourselves to believe that.

When we are born, we are immediately taught that life will eventually pass and that, someday, we will die, because this is what TIME does to you.

We are so conditioned to believe this theory as being the ONLY truth, that we restrict our existence to the very small portion of it that we call "reality"; that same reality that is created by the brain filtered and neuron restrained analysis of the billions of bits of information the Universe(s) showers us with every second.

In that model of existence, Consciousness follows a linear time and participates in an incarnation one life at a time, releasing itself to the beautiful ether of Love after each life.

The problem with this model is that it does not work at the quantum level.
If Consciousness were jumping from one life to the other, taking a break in between, it would not explain, why we couldn't remember our past lives vividly! We still should be able to remember! It's the same Consciousness! Yet we don't or we do but, very seldom remember our "past" lives. Why?

The very reason for that might just be because there is nothing to remember, because nothing happened in the "past"; all happens at the same time!

That would be the most plausible explanation. You cannot remember any "past" life, because there is no "Past" life. They are ALL happening at the same time.

That is indeed my second theory. Consciousness

incarnates in multiple lives, an infinite number of them really, and stays released and free of incarnation, all at the same time. Because Consciousness is within a field of all probabilities and all possibilities, it can collapse any reality into its own by just observing it in the now.

So indeed there is no "remembering" some past lives. All potential lives are different collapsed realities, which are happening at the very same time. And that time is NOW!
But here is the trick: all these realities are at time colliding and interfering with each other, like an electron shot in the double slit somehow becomes a wave of probabilities and interferes with itself!

Time does not matter and we all share the same space. Imagine that all of us are little bubbles, like when you blow bubbles. Sometimes they float by themselves, but sometimes they collide and for a few seconds they get stuck together and become one and then get separated again. Well if all of us are like those little bubbles, that's how we can share sometimes someone else's world or our own world in a different reality, within the same space... For a few second we can hear and see the others or ourselves in the other bubbles and then we separate and we go our own way, though remaining in the same space...

So you see, we do not "remember a past life" we get a glimpse into a parallel reality created by Consciousness.

One piece of evidence of this is what Dr. Brian Weiss mentions in his books and research. Dr. Brian Weiss is

the bestseller author of "Many lives, many masters" a riveting book of his experience as a psychiatrist. After accidentally "regressing" a patient beyond the point of birth, Dr. Weiss embarked on a life-altering journey that would open his mind to the full potential of Consciousness.
What Dr. Weiss did is that not only did he "regress" patients of his, not only did he access his patients' "Past lives" but he also accessed his patients' "Future lives" in what he calls Future Life Progression.

By accessing lives in any linear direction, especially in the future, it tends to suggest that in fact, at the quantum level all what happens is just accessing the field of information and possibilities, which is not linked with time but is available NOW.

Dr. Eben Alexander in his book entitled Proof of Heaven, states that as soon as he was detached of his body and was pure Consciousness, he had absolutely no recollection, no knowledge of his life on Earth. When we look at this type of NDE experience in particular, what would be the most logical, the easiest reason to fathom? That something, some how makes us "forget" our life? So quickly? And for what reason? Or would it be more plausible that because we are everywhere at the same time, we live an infinite number of lives at the same time, we cannot indeed be aware of multiple lives at the same time, otherwise it would be totally confusing and impossible to deal with.

And it's only when there is a glitch in the system or when we are really trying to become the observer that we can get a glimpse of what's happening in a parallel reality of ours. Hence the "past life regression" or the "future life progression" which are in reality "parallel lives states".

CHAPTER 17

Of movement, time and entanglement

As I am pondering upon the past, present and future, there is one inevitable question.
What is this time that constraints our reality and makes it appear chronological.
What is time?

We know time, because we see our planet revolving around itself, creating the illusion of night and day. We have determined that this movement of our planet creates a chronological sequence of events that we have decided to call time.

And it works fairly well; we also revolve around the sun and can quantify that movement into the same unit of time that we use for our own planet self-revolution.

Then we have noticed that pictures taken of the far Universe(s) at different "times" show differences on a same object, clearly indicating movement. Thus, we have determined by mathematical process that time must be involved in those changes as well.

Now, think of this.

What if the Universe(s) stood still? No movement what so ever. Think of it hard and try to imagine.

How would you know of time?

The concept of time is clearly linked to the concept of movement. Without movement there is no time. If all material bodies ceased to move relatively to others, there would not be any frame of reference anymore.

If the Universe(s) stood still, time would cease to exist!

Now, think of each and every infinite number of "nanosecond" of your life. Each "moment" of your life is a still photo of your reality; another moment and another and another one immediately replaces the "previous" one. But each one of those moments is still.

So in fact, your life is just a succession of still moments in which time does not exist.
Again, your life is made of an infinite number of realities intrinsically linked to one another. But does time really link them all?

Einstein clearly showed in his equation E=mc2 that time is a major component in the production of energy as c represents the speed of light. We measure speed by calculating a distance covered in a certain amount of time.
But if time is non-existent, time = 0, and distance can be covered instantly, the equation results in an infinite amount of energy.

And wouldn't an infinite amount of energy be exactly what Consciousness is?
The power of creation and destruction; the power of being omnipotent everywhere, with the same amount of possibilities to the infinite? Or, as I like to put it ॐ=mc2!

Time = 0 is a very difficult notion to apprehend and will most likely remain a barrier to go over if we want to understand the Universe(s) we live in.

But the absence of time or instantaneous measurement effect at a distance, or as Einstein called it: "*spukhafte Fernwirkung* "*spukhafte Fernwirkung*" (spooky action at a distance), isn't that precisely what Quantum physics has succeeded to demonstrate in quantum entanglement?

John Stewart Bell demonstrated quantum entanglement in 1964 when he took on the EPR paradox (Einstein, Podolsky, Rosen paradox), a thought experiment that attempted to show that quantum mechanical theory was incomplete.
He proceeded to introduce the notion of non-local reality by showing that local realism was no longer sufficient to explain measurements of some entangled system.
For the first time, it was demonstrated that a pair of entangled systems would reveal the same measurement regardless of the distance, instantly; which means it would have to happen faster than the speed of light. And as we "know" the speed of light is the maximum known speed in the Universe(s). So it made no sense to classical physics. But it did for

quantum mechanics!

Bell succeeded in showing that time and distance did not matter, that two entangled systems (two electrons, two photons, two small molecules etc…) would present the same results of measurements. If one were observed, the other entangled particle would react instantly showing the same properties than the first one.

If entangled particles can react to each other regardless of distance and time it opens a huge window of supposition for our Consciousness to be able to receive information instantly from another Consciousness. All we need to do is create the connection, the entanglement.

I firmly believe that Quantum Mechanics and its derived future studies will be a key component in explaining Consciousness and its many ramifications.

CHAPTER 18

Getting more attuned, getting "entangled" - Meditation

My life had taken me from the West Coast to the East Coast where I finally decided to create my very own company with no strings attached to any other corporation or anyone else!
Time had finally come for me to spread my very own wings without the protective net of partners, who most of the time had revealed themselves to be more a burden than an added safety net anyway.

I was working really hard at developing my small business in event planning using the full extent of my left brain capacity during the day but was always happy to come home to my dogs, to relax and read.

It was the time when I could not read enough books. I kept buying books by the dozen. Books about spirituality, books about science and quantum physics, books about self-empowerment through meditation, books about spiritual mediums and their journey, books about NDE (Near Death Experiences), books about life after death, books about past life regressions, books on everything that would talk precisely or remotely about Consciousness and its continuum after what we call death.

I would watch any and all documentaries on the Science Channel about the Universe(s) and its evolution, about quantum physics, about unexplained phenomena.

My thirst for left brain knowledge was insatiable.

That is when I discovered the power of meditation.

It all started as a way to control my stress and anxiety due to being a young entrepreneur having to deal with owning my business and making sure it would be successful in order to sustain the few employees I had and myself and guarantee that the INS would extend my business visa, otherwise I would have to go back "home".

But home was no longer France. I hadn't felt better at home than the first day I had set foot in San Francisco and breathed the eucalyptus infused air of the Bay Area right after crossing the beautiful Golden Gate bridge.

So the stakes were high for me and it brought an added stress to my everyday endeavor in making my company successful.

The INS was clear; if the company were not successful the visa would not be renewed down the road.

It was curious though as it felt like life was purposely throwing at me all kinds of obstacles to make me realize I really needed to slow down and rethink my life, rethink my attitude towards others, rethink my ways of coping with stress (smoking cigarettes and drinking coke all day)…

My unhealthy habits combined with my constant reading finally met on mutual ground and gave birth to a solution that became totally obvious: Meditation!

I learned how to slow down and breathe. I learned that when you focus on your breathing, you stop thinking and you start being. I learned meditating helped me connect with Consciousness on command, rather than connections being thrown at me without my consent or invitation.

I learned that I could actually control my left and right brain and decide which one was supposed to be active and which one was supposed to sleep for a while.

It became a habit and it helped me go through a rough patch of professional and personal incidents that decided to accumulate from January 2000 to mid 2005.

But in fact meditation did more than that. Using different kinds of technique (guided meditations, self meditations, visualization meditations, chakras meditations) I kept training my right brain to open up to receive the data from the informational Universe(s). I became more and more confident with my visions, and sensory perceptions.

I started to completely trust the process of letting go, connecting with Consciousness and letting in information.

Some information became too strong, too intense to keep for myself and I started to share with my friends and family, giving my very first experimental readings.

I was able to now completely control what and who would come in and to close at any given time. It was a huge change from my previous experiences that had seemed so imposed on me.

Meditation helped me find the right track and is still today the only natural way I know that will allow me to attain the necessary altered state of Consciousness for connecting with other souls, incarnated or not.

I remember a particular reading I did for someone and his sister whom I was close at the time. Their mother had passed way before I knew them and I virtually knew nothing about her other than her way of passing and her name.
It was one of my very first deliberate readings and I still felt very awkward doing this but I tried hard to let go.

I sat at the table in front of them and started to breathe deeply. I had meditated before hand but stage fright was trying to bring me back to my awake state, calling my left brain desperately to rationalize the whole situation.

But I fought hard and was able to bring myself back to that fine line where you instantly feel that you are connected, that you have grabbed the signal line, as CRV people would say. It is very difficult to explain the sensation when you have grabbed it. But when you

143

have, then <u>information starts pouring</u>.

I came up with a few elements of their childhood and then I heard the word: perfume. Immediately, the vision of an oblong shaped perfume bottle came to my mind with purple colors flashing.
When I told them about my vision, the sister was in awe. She said her mother was wearing this perfume called "Poison" by Christian Dior, which comes in an oblong purple bottle. But the interesting part is not that I had captured the perfume, but that it brought back a very distinct memory about her mother and her.
When the sister was pregnant, she could not stand that perfume, it made her nauseated and it had been a big story between her and her mother.
The perfume was clearly a way from her mother to validate it was her connecting and communicating!

You have to remember, this was one of my first readings. I was amazed myself at the details I was receiving. But I still did not know how to articulate and formulate all this.
Why would she come up with the perfume and not something else? I don't know and I am glad I did not try to explain my vision, because in fact the raw delivery of material made it ten times more powerful for my sitter.
I remember that being caught into my own amazement at the process, I lost the signal line. In the same way it is difficult to explain how one feels when one is connected, it is equally hard to convey the feeling of being disconnected. You just sense it.
It feels like waking up from a light sleep and starting hearing your surroundings again.

So I started to breathe deeply again, and closed by eyes. When I felt connected again, that's when it happened.

I heard a very distinct word in my mind's ears. A word that meant absolutely nothing! Because I had never heard this word in any of the three languages I knew, I decided to keep silent.

I discovered then that when a person on the other side wants you to say something, she does not let go until you do.

Ensued a battle in my mind. The fight was between my left brain that had decided I was not going to make a fool of myself saying something I had never heard before - after all I did not even know if this was even a word! - And the energy connecting with me, now pounding me with the word, repeating it over and over.

Eventually it became so loud in my head, I had to abdicate and say it.

The effect it had on my sitters was totally unexpected!

I thought I had just ruined my non-existent reputation as a medium by saying something so ridiculously devoid of meaning.

In fact it did the complete opposite. The brother gasped for air and said, "Oh my God, this is the brand of art drawing furniture that my mom was using!"

They were both from Norway and the mother had a hobby of painting. The brand was a Norwegian brand. No wonder I had no clue about what I was saying!

It was then that I realized I could not let my left brain interfere with my readings anymore. On the contrary I really had to shut it down completely embracing and fully trusting the information my right brain was receiving with no fear of being "ridicule" or "wrong".

My interpretation could totally be wrong if I tried to interpret things with my own frame of reference, which is different from anyone else's frame of reference. But the raw information captured from the signal line, or from the other Consciousness connecting with me was to be trusted as true and valid.

I totally understood that it would be a struggle to work towards total annihilation of left brain power during readings, but I also realized it was the only way I could create a safe haven for valid exchanges with people's loved ones.

At that point meditation became a part of my daily life. I always say: "Working with your brain is like working with a muscle, the more you train it, the better it responds to stimuli and the better it performs!"

CHAPTER 19

Is Meditation the only way to attain an altered state of Consciousness?

Meditation is the most natural, simplest and cheapest way to get to the necessary altered state of Consciousness that will allow connection with the informational Universe(s) and retrieving information from it. But is it the only way?
Can we induce the same state with technology, in a controlled environment?

The answer is yes.

An altered-state of Consciousness is a state that is different from your regular "awake" state called Beta state.

There are several states of Consciousness.

Beta state is when you are fully awake, fully aware of your surroundings and capable of functioning during your regular daily activities be it working or eating or exercising or having fun.

Beta state can be determined on an electro-encephalogram (EEG) by measuring the brain activity or brain waves. The frequency of Beta state is usually measured between 12Hz and 38Hz with subcategories of low Beta, Beta and high Beta.

Beta and Gamma waves (27Hz and up) are also associated with creative thinking, concentration, problem solving, language; all of which are performed mainly by our left brain. As I am writing this now, my brain is most likely surfing full throttle on Gamma waves!

Then there is the Alpha state (8Hz to 12Hz). This is a state that you are trying to achieve with light meditation; state in which you are relaxed with not much thinking, not much processing information with your left brain. A state you will recognize yourself in when you wake up in the morning or you are about to fall asleep.
This is an excellent state for mediumship, CRV and ESP.

You are still awake but "not here".

From Alpha you can drift to Theta (3Hz to 8Hz). Theta is the sate of light sleep or extreme total relaxation. When you are in Theta state your right brain is ready to receive information without having your left brain interfere with it. This is the best state for mediumship and OBE (Out of body experience).

After Theta comes Delta (0.2Hz to 3Hz). In Delta state you are in a deep dreamless sleep. Awareness is gone. Your Consciousness is no longer filtered by your brain. Your brain has shut down all cognitive perceptions to let your primal functions repair, restore your entire body.
With deep meditation you can achieve Alpha and even Theta waves. Practice is the key. Choose a very relaxing, soothing music that does not contain too many instruments. Make sure you are comfortable sitting in a love seat or laying down and close your eyes listening to the music.
Use Pranayama breathing which is a method of breathing where you inhale through your nose counting up to what's comfortable for you (eight seconds was a good start for me), hold the air for a couple of seconds and then start exhaling, controlling the flow or air during the amount of time you inhaled, contracting your abdominal muscles at the end of the exhalation. Pause for a couple of seconds, relax the abdomen and repeat, constantly until your brain stops thinking and all you can "think about" is your breathing and feeling more and more relaxed...
That is basic relaxation to start any meditation process. To get to Alpha and Theta state you can use this technique followed by a guided meditation or you can trick your brain by listening to special sounds!

There are studies that show that listening to certain type of white noises will trigger the brain to enter a certain state.
The theory behind those studies is that sending a pulsating sound with a certain frequency will resonate with the brain, which in return will have the tendency

to align its own frequency with the one it has received; hence inducing certain Consciousness states. This process is called entrainment.

You can practice entrainment at home with CDs that will play white noises emulating Alpha and Theta waves and it might be an easy way for beginner meditators to "feel" when they are in those states once they are ready to try it with meditation only.

But some people push the envelope even further.
It is believed that a certain type of sounds called binaural beats are capable of taking you much further than simple Alpha and Theta states by triggering an OBE (Out of Body Experience) where you can actually connect with your loved ones who have passed.

This is what the Monroe Institute does with its research on binaural beats.
When you visit the Monroe Institute website, this is what you read on its front page:

- The Monroe Institute (TMI) is a non-profit research and educational organization dedicated to enhancing the uses and understanding of human Consciousness.
- We are not affiliated with any religion, philosophy, or spiritual practice.
- We ask only that you consider the possibility that you are more than your physical body.

This is exactly my philosophy. We do not need to bring religion and spiritual practices in our quest of

understanding and using the full extent of our Consciousness.
Consciousness is intrinsically part of the Universe(s). It might even be what holds it together and creates it at any given moment. That my daughter wants to call it God Consciousness gives me the feeling that this is what it is; a pretty darn amazing thing that is able to create realities when observing around.

Robert Monroe a famous radio broadcaster, music composer and smart business man decided in 1956 to set up a research about how to improve and learn things during deep sleep using several types of sound patterns.

Using himself as the experimenter, Mr. Monroe experienced a life changing sets of events while listening to those sounds and coined the term "Out of Body Experience" OBE that today has become mainstream in the field of Consciousness research.

After researching and refining the method, Mr. Monroe created the Monroe Institute to further perfect the protocol of research and allow people to also experience what he had himself been given to discover.

Using Binaural beats among other types of sound patterns, experimenters can today spend a few days to a few weeks at the center and get deeper into the discovery of their own Consciousness.

Binaural beats are the resultant frequency generated by the broadcasting of one sound with one frequency in one ear, and another sound with another frequency in the other year. The difference between the two frequencies creates a binaural beat.

What is important here is that the difference is not registered by our ears but is registered by our brain and by doing so creates in our brain an altered state of Consciousness inducing the same results as deep meditation and even possible OBEs.

After those experiences, the experimenters recount being able to feel a deep connection with the Universe(s) and even connecting with their deceased loved ones, coming back from the altered state with tangible validations and messages received by them.

Whether we use meditation, white noise and binaural beats the method seems to be the same. <u>Inducing an Alpha and Theta state in our brain allows for a deep connection and opens the flow of information</u>.

Because our brain has such a limited perception of the informational Universe(s), the more we step away from its left aptitude, the better!

We cannot of course do without our brain, but we can at least try to use its full right brain capacity of sensory perceptions to better ourselves in understanding our world.

CHAPTER 20

Going back to this "other life"

From the first glimpses of my expanding Consciousness in my childhood to the spontaneous, uncontrolled windows opened through the veil during my 20's to finally reaching the point where I understood I could not only control all this but constantly improve my connections, the journey had taken me on three different continents, many human relationships, lots of ups and downs and tons of soul searching moments.

But I was now on a path that I could not stop.

As my company was trying to recover from the aftermath of 9/11, I was struggling personally and professionally to keep my nose above the water level.

I was dealing with so many issues at the same time that it felt that sometimes I had put my body on autopilot while my mind was trying to tackle every single hurdle thrown at me.

I literally had to detach myself from the reality I knew, otherwise I would have lost said mind!

From keeping the company afloat and trying to maintain my employees' jobs, to dealing with a crumbling marriage that was totally draining my life force, and fighting some old broken heart demons that kept harassing me, it was tough.

I would only find solace in reading and meditating and doing séances for others. When I was able to make a connection for someone, it would bring me so much joy and peace in the midst of my own turmoil.

One day, I decided it was time to revisit my vision, the one that spontaneously came to me on that plane to San Francisco. I knew there was more to that story and I wanted to finish it. I knew somehow it had meaning and I had to find it.

As much as I had trained myself to connect to other people's Consciousness, I had no idea how to get to a parallel life of mine. So I enrolled the help of professional hypnotist Diane Ross, M.A.

Diane Ross is a wonderful lady who has dedicated her life to the study and practice of NLP and hypnosis.

As Irene Struif LMHC, BS, Reiki Master, CH, NLP puts it:

"Neurolinguistic Programming (NLP) is a technology of human behavior that can be used to help people eliminate unwanted behaviors, acquire new skills or make other important changes. NLP is also about learning how to run your brain, rather than letting it randomly run you, to get the results you want for yourself."

As I sat on Diane's comfortable recliner at her practice, listening to relaxing music, I did not feel like a stranger to the method. After all I was doing this myself all the time.

But this time was going to be different. With her soft yet reassuring voice, Diane started to take me through a certain number of places before I was able to start the jumps from one moment of my life to another; until she felt I was ready to make the big jump, to cross that threshold, the moment of birth.

As I am going through what I call a "flash of bright light" I immediately find my self on that street again. Wearing that same light blue dress, with that same hotel to my right and those same three oak trees to my left, walking on that unique sandy road that goes though that western town in 1882.

Again, I relive the scene where I see my husband being killed by those three guys.
But before I could jump to that fateful scene where I commit suicide killing my self with a gun to my head, Diane takes me further and deeper asking me to have a good look at myself and at my husband.

That's when I remember "I am pregnant! Oh my god I am pregnant!"

And as I look at the man, my husband on the ground, I feel anger against him instead of compassion and love! I also realize that that man has the same soul as a former flame who caused me lots of heartache.

But why?

Sensing something had to give, Diane took me ever so gently deeper asking me to find out why I decided to kill myself.

This is when I suddenly found myself sitting in the tall grass of a riverbank feeling a nice gentle breeze on my cheeks, feeling totally happy. Next to me, with the same smile and radiant beauty that happiness brings in people, was sitting the love of my life, a Lakota Sioux young man called Matuka. His long dark hair was floating in the wind and we were laughing and just being happy, together. Our love and happiness had transcended the time and the fact we were from two different worlds, two different cultures, and two different races. It did not even occur to us that all this existed. We just loved each other period.

I was sitting in Diane's chair, I knew I was present in this chair, but my Consciousness was totally gone, from that space/time moment. I was reliving the whole thing. And it felt so good. I felt so happy at a deeper level of Consciousness it is almost impossible to describe. It contrasted so much with the hardship I had been going through for a while that it was pure bliss.

Unfortunately this beautiful moment was suddenly and abruptly disrupted by a band of horsemen charging into us, screaming and yelling. I was terrified. Matuka stood up to protect me, but one of the men, pointed his riffle right at him and shot him dead right in front of me.

And as the unthinkable happens, I understand that they had been sent to do exactly that, as words had come to my family that I was in love with a Native American man and that was the absolute sin.

Back to Diane's office, I am in my chair, sobbing uncontrollably releasing the pain that had been within me for so long. Even as a child, I wanted to be one of them so bad, if you remember. All I wanted was my grand father to build me teepees, to dress like a Native American, to have bows and arrows and "fight" the cowboys.
But again, remember, I was born and raised in France, not the US.

This pain had been in and with me since the beginning and the release of it was an unbelievable moment of truth. It was like being reborn.

As Diane lets me grieve for my love, she gently takes me away from that scene and asks me why I married the sheriff then.

I come to understand that my family discovering that I was pregnant with Matuka's child decided to marry me to this man to "cover up"; and that I was so disinterested in my life at this point that I just did what they asked me to do. I was feeling so empty.
The sheriff took good care of me, but I never loved him.

Yet, when he got killed too, it was too much for me to bear and I decided to kill myself on top of a hill on Indian ground.

Because Matuka's family knew about us and had no prejudice, they went and retrieved my body and placed it on a scaffold in a traditional burial ceremony.

I also found out that my dad was part of the railway construction in the area, that lead to San Francisco.

The story had been finished, and the missing pieces of the puzzle had been found and put in place.

It also contributed to reinforce the interpretation of many factors of my life:
- My love for Native Americans from a very young age,
- That fear of the gun when my ex's brother was given the potential opportunity to use it to commit suicide,
- My career path shifting from science to hospitality (I owned a hotel in that other life)
- Why everything in my life pushed me to move to the US and specifically to the West and San Francisco first.
- The reason why the man who caused me so much heartache in this life being indeed my surrogate husband in that other life, had told me the day he broke up with me that he did not think I was made to have children; when the subject of creating a family had not even been brought up before.

Had he asked me I would have told him I wanted to find and be sure to be with the right person; that on the contrary, I wanted to have children, more than he could ever imagine. But clearly his soul too knew at a deeper level that I had killed myself while being pregnant, and in his mind that made me an unfit mother.

Every single moment of my life that had had a clear impact on me, could be traced back to this life of which I had been given the chance to revisit the decisive moments, twice!

The renewed knowledge I was given thanks to that tapping into one of my parallel lives helped understand better why I was going through what I was going through.

I realized the power of NLP, meditation and self-hypnosis was far greater than I had ever imagined.

CHAPTER 21

What do we learn from our parallel lives?

Being able to tap into your parallel life is like being handed a manual on how to tackle your own actual life:

- The parallel life you jump into at a particular time in your life seems to fit what you are going through at that very moment,
- I teaches you how to handle the same obstacles,
- How to react differently to hardship and depression,
- How to know who you will be close to and who will understand you,
- And logically how to stay away from the ones who will take you down and will not understand you for who you are,
- How to follow the flow and trust the Universe(s), knowing that everything has meaning.

What I had just done with the regression was giving me a broad view of what could be achieved.

It opened my mind even more to the obvious: Our Consciousness was ONE and yet infinitely divisible in the many life scenarios needed to achieve total comprehension.

This is when I became more and more interested in the quantum world and its multiple possibilities.

ONE!

What if the Universe(s) was just an infinite number of lives superimposed like a mosaic forming a grand scaled image representing your Consciousness in its totality? Each part of the mosaic by itself would not represent much but yet, if one piece of the mosaic were missing, the image would be incomplete.

Visiting a parallel life is not just a fun thing to do and should not be taken too lightly. It is a very profound act of self-discovery that helps understanding oneself at one's deepest core level.

This idea of parallel lives versus past or future lives also helps answer the question that every true skeptic always asks:
"There are more and more people on Earth and if when we die we do reincarnate, how do you explain the ever growing population?"

The answer is very simple. If you take our Consciousness as a whole made of an infinite number of potential materializations, it is more than probable than we can incarnate in two or more lives at any given time, hence the number of growing population that does not reflect the number of "Consciousness" in the Universe(s).

And then again, one reality is detached from the other with no recollection of what our higher Consciousness is except when we are giving ourselves the proper brain training to attain that level, or state, and retrieve information from it.

Consider your Consciousness as the matrix of yourself and every single life you incarnate a vector of that matrix.
This is why I decided that with the knowledge of my many different vectors of incarnations, I could most likely choose the best for me in the one incarnation I was conscious to be in.

And I went back to Diane's office!

This time with a very specific purpose in mind: Stop smoking!

Once again I found myself reclining on Diane's chair with a nice blanket on me to keep me warm. When you let go of everything and relax, your body temperature goes down and there is nothing more annoying than being cold when you are trying so hard to detach yourself from Earthly occurrences.

I had bought three one-hour sessions with Diane to quit smoking. That's how sure she was that it would be sufficient to achieve just that.

While in deep relaxation she took me through a certain number of visualizations and it was time to implement NLP.

We first chose a body trigger to help me kill in the egg the urge of picking up a cigarette. She suggested I touch my ear each time I wanted to take a cigarette and keep that gesture as the trigger for my brain to stop the urge.

Once the session was over, I came back home and tried it a few times. I was very unsuccessful. I did not pick a cigarette, but it was more because of my willpower than anything else, like when you start a diet. I was struggling.
I knew though that in the long run, this would not work.

So I went back for my second session and explained to Diane, that the body trigger was not good for me, I needed something more profound, something that would impact my soul, not my body.

This is when she radically changed the NLP and we together decided to use some future life progression therapy.

As I was sitting on the chair, instead of having me going to the point I need to take a cigarette and choose a trigger movement to stop it, she took me on a path.

On that path, I encountered a fork.
From that fork, the path that went to the left was one version, possibility, of my life, with me smoking in it; and the path that went to the right was another possibility or version of my life, with me being smoking free.

163

She gently engaged me to the left path and took me through my entire life, there, as a powerless witness of my auto destruction. I do not remember all the details, but what I do remember very vividly are the prominent grey and dark colors associated with this life.

Everything was grey, there was no color, no happiness; it was like living in a constant fog, alone and growing increasingly sick and sad. And knowing that I was the main actor, the main contributor and the main perpetrator of this dark world to myself made me even sadder and angry. I felt like the hermit in the Tarot cards, walking a lonely path, with no light. My mouth was dry, and I eventually declined to the point of dying alone miserably.

All along, Diane did not suggest one bit of these visions, she just prompted me to go on and push forward, looking at myself and feeling the emotions associated with that path.

It was extremely terrifying.

Then she took me back to the fork and had me start my journey to the right path, the "right path" and the path with no smoking. Immediately everything lit up. Amazing bright and vibrant colors were all around me. I was not walking on that path; I was dancing, twirling, with a huge smile on my face. There were flowers everywhere, and I was singing. It reminds me of the movie "What dreams may come". Both worlds you see in the movie actually resembled a lot what I saw on each path, though totally free from religious judgment. My journey on the path went on and I could see myself having two wonderful children, and somehow I disappeared in the colors, I blended with them and became part of the light. It was just pure bliss!

When the session was over, I was shaken to say the least.
It was extremely powerful.

When I came home, the next time I felt the urge to take a cigarette, I closed my eyes and placed myself at the fork.
Instantly my brain shifted and the urge went away, without struggling or consciously fighting the urge.
I had conquered the addiction.

It was over.

I went in for my third session just as reinforcement, but I can truly honestly say I was done by the second one.

Because I was given a glimpse into another possibility of me, I was able to create my own reality the way I wanted it for this incarnation I was aware of consciously.
I learned from my quantum me what would help me grow and help me fight an Earthly addiction.

But what if we don't learn?

I can only speak from my own experience and I know it is not enough to create a precedent as the base of a possible theory, but the many similarities between the life I am conscious of living in as I write this book and the one I had a glimpse of in my lucid dream and regression make me wonder why there are so many repeated themes.

If we take the point of view of the skeptic, wouldn't it

be easier to explain all this by a self auto-suggested release dream in which all that bothered me or marked me in a psychological significant way in my life found its way from deep down my psyche to the surface in order for me to better cope with all these underlying issues; rather than me having a glimpse into a parallel life existing with as much possibilities and probabilities as the one I am conscious of living in now?

Frankly, I don't see why. If we take, just for a minute, the time to extract ourselves from our very own little bubble on Earth and look into the eyes of the Universe(s), or dive into the abyss of the infinite small in the quantum world and witness what happens there in terms of non local reality, I say there is a fair chance that the second proposition of my repeated experience be true.

In that case then, why? Why would we be allowed to get to see one or more of our infinite lives? I should not say "allowed" though as it implies that a higher power gives us permission to do so, I should say: why can we see one or more of our infinite lives? Is it a glitch in the system? Or is it purposely, so that we can learn from each other's possibility and change the outcome in each one of them?

Isn't nature by observation just an amazing evolution based on trial and error?

That's what nature does. Nature tries. It works? It continues and reproduces. It does not? It stops in that direction and takes another one!

The Universe(s) is the same, I am sure there have been many attempts at creating matter, before having what we can observe today. And it's a continuous process, never stopping!
Nature learns from itself, the Universe(s) learns from itself, we learn from ourselves.

So seeing one particular possibility of life helps my higher Consciousness create an optimum set of experiences to be inspired by in another one.

That is why past life regression and future life progression, two faces of the same coin called parallel realities, are so successful in psychotherapy!

As discussed prior in the chapter called "**Past life regression, reincarnation, or is it really in the past?**" the work of Dr. Brian Weiss among others is compelling in that sense.

CHAPTER 22

Getting in touch with the After Life and Consciousness research community

In the very early 2000's, my passion for the matter of Life after Death kept growing and my work as a business owner kept increasing. It was very difficult to manage the two together.

I was doing more and more readings, but because of my lifestyle, working really hard days, week ends, and sometimes long evenings and travelling all over, it was difficult to find the necessary time to set aside for meditation and readings.

I felt frustrated because the passion I had was turning more into a calling and I could not give it the time needed to grow.

The more I was working with my passion the less I felt excited about my event planning work. Reading for people was always about sharing love, compassion and finding closure.
 It was all about sharing emotions and helping others, using our human ability of empathy. I was totally in my element there. At work, it was the complete

opposite, everything had become all about money, being the cheapest, the more competitive, regardless of the effort or the love you were putting into your work.

Call me selfish, but the absolute lack of recognition for a job well done in my business, by increasingly voracious and deal hungry corporate clients made me sad and sick to my stomach. The absence of human relationship, which existed even a few years before had become a daily occurrence and was leaving me in disarray and empty.

When I was doing readings, the feeling of being useful, and being a little help for others in their grief was so much more rewarding than the money making corporate world.

The gap between my two activities grew increasingly bigger and bigger to the point where I was feeling a violent repulsion for the job I was doing and it was time for a change.

I started to think that there was a lot of research done in the area of Consciousness and life after death, but they were scattered. There were a lot of talks about science and spirituality but they were not organized. There was a lot of work done by wonderful true mediums and sensitives but they were not recognized as part of a profound paradigm shift in our society or still treated like entertainment.

I then figured that if I could put my work and experience in event planning to work I could potentially come up with the 1st convention for Life after Death regrouping everyone involved (Doctors, Scientists, Religious and spiritual figures, Mediums).

I started researching the Internet for all the people I wanted to contact.

I made a very long list including:
Psychic Medium John Edward, Psychic Medium John Holland, Psychic Medium Suzan Northrop, Dr. Gary Schwartz (author of The After Life Experiments), Dr. Melvin Morse, Dr. Raymond Moody, The Dalai Lama, Bill Guggenheim just to name a few.

I tried to find their email addresses and then wrote a long email that I sent to each one of them hoping to trigger an interest. I wanted to create a convention that would gather all sources of research and experimentation within the community of Consciousness.

The idea was to once a year share the work done in all directions be it scientific, spiritual, grief counseling and come up with ideas and protocols for new research to come, to further advance our knowledge of Consciousness, its ramifications and the use that could be done with it to do good.

The first ones to answer were the office of the Dalai Lama, Psychic Medium John Holland, Bill Guggenheim and Dr. Gary Schwartz. The office of the Dalai Lama thanked me for my email, acknowledged the good idea but nicely turned me down.
Dr. Gary Schwartz, psychic medium John Holland and Bill Guggenheim were the three who answered positively, thinking that the idea was a great one. We

started to exchange with Dr. Schwartz about some ideas, but it unfortunately did not go anywhere.

I think it was too early in the paradigm shift to generate interest at the highest level and my project died in the egg.

About a decade later, Terri Daniels did the exact same thing I tried to do back then with her Afterlife Conference and it is a huge success today. Bringing on board people such as Dr Eben Alexander III or Dr Joe O'Connell who have seen their shares of life and death events in the ER or the operating room, as speakers, clearly shows that there is a shift in the paradigm regarding Consciousness and it makes me very happy!

Eventually my decision to stop organizing for the corporate world came served to me on a platter when I met my second husband and we decided to create a family.

The birth of my first child literally came as deliverance for me.
I gladly put my business to the side and focused on my new job as a mom, but still doing readings, still increasing my knowledge in all matters of Consciousness.

CHAPTER 23

Meeting with Gary Reece, NDE experiencer

What is an NDE? You must have heard this term many times if you are interested in the subject matter of Life after Death or the Continuum of Consciousness. NDE (Near Death Experience) happens when someone dies, experiences events while dead, and then is brought back to life to talk about it.

The term Near Death Experience should actually be changed to Death Experience, because, people who go through that process, really die in medical terms.

What's dying? Well on a medical point of you, you are dead when your heart has ceased beating and your brain has flat lined too. No heart beat, no brain activity. It is said that after five minutes of no heartbeat and blood flow to the brain, the brain cells start to die irreversibly.
In other words your body is shutting down to the point where "conscious" thinking and normal brain functions are totally impossible.

Depending on the culture, Death has been considered either the end of everything, or the beginning of eternal life. In the Aborigine's culture in Australia, life is actually a dream state and death represents the real life…

Since the human race has been able to feel emotions, death has been revered, feared or embraced.

But in all cases, death represents the loss of the body, as we know it, and that's why in most cultures, the body is disposed of, either buried, or cremated, dumped in the sea or left to decay by natural elements.

And in most cultures while the body is disposed of, the "soul" is accompanied with much prayers to a supposed heaven or an after life realm.

So how do we reconcile these beliefs and what people experience when they have an NDE? And How do we reconcile this and science?

What is the point of view of a good portion of the medical field about NDE and OBE (Out of Body Experiences) and those vivid experiences people have while dead?

There have been many researches on the subject and the medical community seems to attribute those experiences to the release of powerful hormones at the time of death in the brain that triggers vivid hallucinations, hence the NDE and OBE.
Another explanation given is that because most people say that time stops and does not exist while

experiencing those events while dead, they might actually think they are going through these while dead but most likely are going through them as they are regaining Consciousness mistakenly thinking that they are still dead.

I agree that while all NDEs and OBEs might not be attributed to a powerful and profoundly spiritual experience, I have to disagree totally and completely with the unique and restrictive explanation given by the traditional medical community based only on chemical reactions in the brain.

There are multiple reasons for this.

1 – The Medical definition of Consciousness:
Consciousness
A clear state of awareness of self and the environment in which attention is focused on immediate matters, as distinguished from mental activity of an unconscious or subconscious nature.
Mosby's Medical Dictionary, 8th edition. © 2009, Elsevier.

In medical death terms the first thing you lose is your Consciousness. So you clearly have no sense of self or your environment.

How cannot you have any sense of self and your environment when experiencing NDEs and OBEs when people going through this recount clearly seeing their body and having a very vivid and clear sense of living fully the moment.
They also recount their surroundings, the medical team working on them, they recall seeing their body from above and KNOWING it's them.

This is the first contradiction with medical death terms and explanation.

2 – Since Consciousness, subConsciousness and dream state can only exist in medical terms when the brain presents electrical activity, what's the answer to the powerful experiences lived by people going through an NDE when their EEG (ElectroEncephaloGram) is flat or their cortex is so damaged by lack of blood flow or grave illness such as meningitis that there is zero chance of Consciousness as defined by modern medicine? Another medical contradiction…

Until very recently, I always believed that the term clinically dead meant that both EEG (Electro Encephalogram) and EKG (Electro Cardiogram) had to be flat. No brain activity, no heartbeat: death.

Dr. Eben Alexander III a neurosurgeon who had his own brush with death and a very powerful NDE made it clear it is not that.

Listening to Dr. Eben Alexander III at one of his conferences made me realize that in fact, we are dead as long as what makes the essence of us is no longer here i.e. when the brain is no longer functioning, responding, and capable of processing Consciousness. The heart can beat as long as it wants, but if the brain has become a soup, it's death.
Even if we come back, once the brain has been destroyed, the chances of being able to recover "Consciousness" are slim to none. And brain cells start dying after four to five minutes without blood flow…

In the case of Dr. Eben Alexander, with a rare E.Coli meningitis, his brain "should" not have recuperated the way it did. After seven days in a deep coma, with a raging infection that had taken over his entire cortex, he should not have been able let alone to come back, but to recuperate ALL his faculties. It was just a pure miraculous recovery. From Dr. Alexander's point of view, even if his heart did not stop beating, his brain was damaged enough by the raging infection to declare Death.
They were actually ready to stop all treatment when he came back...

Of course on a Consciousness point of view, his ordeal was and is everything but death. It is quite the opposite in fact. It's the ability for Consciousness to return to a pure wave state, a state with no limitations, where nothing is created, nothing is destroyed, but everything keeps changing to another form, forever and ever (in Earthly time perception).

3- if, as some researches tend to say, those experiences are actually lived by the patient once they regain Consciousness (on a medical point of view), why people going through NDEs recall very specific details that happened in the room they were in while they were actually medically DEAD.
And I am not talking just about hearing (which according to some doctors is the last thing to go), I am talking about images, from people around the hospital bed they are laying on or even in hallways and in some cases even further in the cafeteria where family is waiting, coming back with startling account of things that they've seen and heard from that far away of their death bed...
Another contradiction.

4 – **Now if all of what people are experiencing during and NDE is only due to hallucinations because of lack of oxygen in the brain and the release of Endorphin** in a mechanism of avoidance response and emotional preservation, why can those people recount details on what happened to them while they were clinically dead. If they were hallucinating, while their brain was flat lining, how do they know the name of the doctors who were working on them? How do they know what is said, how do they see their own body worked on recalling all procedures done on them upon return...

Yet NDEs state can apparently be reproduced in experiments using powerful drugs. Yes, people experience out of body experiences and spiritual encounters but can they give details of their surroundings and conversation in the very room they are while undergoing this experiment?

And in any case, while those experiments only prove that some parts of OBEs and NDEs can be reproduced when being medically "alive", they neither disprove nor negate the fact that these experiences happen as well during medical death when the brain is non functional.

5 – **But maybe the most powerful evidence for me is about the memory that these people have of the entire NDE event they experienced**. Again, according to medicine, memory is created by the brain, located in the brain, and stored in the brain.

When a person experiences and NDE during clinical death, how can they "remember" everything to tell the story when they come back if their brain was non functional? In other words how can their brain have

processed all the memories and information of what they saw and heard and felt if there were no brain activity, or if the cortex was destroyed, no connections happening, nothing while they were experiencing them?
And yet another contradiction of the medical explanation...

I am neither a medical doctor, nor do I have any medical academic knowledge, just the basics from life and a strong will to learn, but what I am using here is plain simple LOGIC.

Forget for a moment the spiritual aspect of NDEs, look at them with the most factual, logical mind, you will see that all five points above make complete sense and that the simplest explanation possible for and NDE is that our Consciousness is NOT the product of brain activity but something else.
Brain is just a mere processor of a signal, that's why it has so many connections. It needs to be able to process Consciousness signals and turn them, collapse them, into our created Reality, which is of course a reduction, a filter of what the Universe(s) is.

People who experience NDEs call the event "life altering".

Most of them actually feel they have risen from their body, and report to have seen and heard what the medical team was doing to their body to try to resuscitate it or what was happening around them.
In almost all cases they tell beautiful stories of some sort of spiritual encounter. A tunnel of light is often seen and feelings of peace and happiness are not uncommon. They also report meeting with deceased loved ones and talking to them.

But the most important fact is that when they come back, they REMEMBER everything that happened to them while they were... dead... They can describe perfectly what the medical team did to their body, they describe the procedures, the words that were pronounced, who were there and they recall everything very clearly. Some of them also report conversations they heard and saw between family members waiting in the hospital hall! They report, because they REMEMBER!

This clearly points to the fact that Consciousness and even memory might be located outside the brain, outside the body, not needing the bodily form to exist.

When you watch television, your TV does not create the program you are watching. Your TV is just a receptor that processes a signal that already exists and has traveled quite extensively through space already.
Your dish or antenna captures the signal, relays it to the TV and allows you to be aware of the program you're watching... Well, imagine Consciousness or your soul if you prefer that word, being that signal, it is captured by your body and your brain processes it and interprets it and allows "your Consciousness", the "program" to manifest itself.

If the TV goes dark, the program signal will no longer be processed by it, but the program will still be broadcast out there and the memory of its signal will still be present as a waveform!
In other words the brain might not be what creates Consciousness but rather a tool that Consciousness uses to express itself on Earth, even if the filter of the brain reduces its expression.

Now let's look at the commonalities in NDEs.
The most evident commonalities in NDEs are an instant KNOWLEDGE of being detached, a complete detachment from one's body and whatever is going on with it most of the time accompanied with a sense of floating and seeing one's own body from above, the immense feeling of total well being, bliss and unconditional love and protection, NEVER FELT BEFORE.
With the feeling of Love and Protection comes this clear strong will of NOT going back to the aching body but moving forward towards the light, the beings, or the energy felt calling or pulling the person into that blissful state of awe.

People of any origin, any race, any culture, any religion and any scientific background have experienced NDEs. Almost ALL of them recount not wanting to go back to their body and considering the experience a life altering event that brings major shifts and changes in one's way of seeing life and living it.

They are no longer afraid of dying, what a beautiful gift!

On a show about real life stories of people having NDEs and recounting them, called "I survived beyond and back", airing on Bio.com TV (on Sunday, august 7th 2011) an Internal Medicine Doctor called "Bob" tells his story about having a heart attack and dying at the hospital while his colleagues are trying to resuscitate him. He has the most powerful experience while clinically dead seeing three lights and KNOWING instantly they were his passed dad, friend and a young boy that had died the week prior. He recalls emotionally the feeling of Love and the wish of letting himself go into this blissful state. Even though in his own words he says it is very difficult for him, as a medical doctor to admit this, he feels like he had a divine experience. It is the only word he can think about.

If a medical doctor, with all his knowledge admits that what he went through is beyond what medicine could explain, why are we even questioning the matter still?

One night, during a party my husband and I were lucky to meet new friends.

Gary was among them and we had a good time talking appreciating his down to Earth sense of humor.

One day, I got word that our friend Gary had been in the hospital for a very serious condition. The whole community started to send positive energy towards him, as his prognosis was very grave. Then something terrible and incredible at the same time happened.

Our friend died.

The crazy part is that he did not die from his condition, but from a massive allergic reaction to iodine during a test at the hospital he was in for his illness.

But the beauty of it all is that, after being gone for five and a half minutes, he came back.

We were all ecstatic that he had pulled through but still very worried as the condition he went in for was extremely life threatening. But he made it and actually in a way that was nothing short of a miracle!

Knowing him as such a down to Earth guy, I wanted to know if he experienced anything while he was gone. And to my amazement, he did.

So I asked him if he would accept a formal interview with me, so that I could relate his experience on my website for others to read.
Below is the interview I had with him:

"So Gary, tell us a little about yourself (your age, what kind of person you are, what you do, your spiritual and scientific inclinations)
I am 57 years young, I am a straight talker, joker, like to make people feel good, don't like closed narrow-minded people, free spirited but at the same time like order. I work at the Sanford Orlando airport on planes; also work at Walmart as all around fixer and assembler of anything mechanical, I have a BSc in Engineering and an MSc in Aerospace Engineering. I love to take things apart and put things together, I am not religious in the traditional sense. I think that we move on to a different plane at a different level, like the Hindus feel about moving on. Guess I'll find out one day. I am a firm believer in science but blended with faith.

What happened to you when you felt ill and needed to go to the hospital, what were the symptoms?

I found that one day I ran short of breath on a walk from my van to work office. Two days later I saw my doctor about it. My doctor did an EKG and sent me to a cardiologist; he found sixteen blood clots in my heart (one was through the top two chambers and blocking the valves).

I would have a heart attack or it would break off and go to my brain; [The doctor] said I had a good chance of dying, [The doctor said I had] many in my lungs, and one large one in my leg, he said if I went home I would die.
Doctors had no idea why, where or how these came from, and sent me straight to the cardiology ICU. They started treatment, and did a CAT scan. Next morning I had an endoscope put down my throat to look at my heart, next was the CT scan.

While in this they injected one pint of iodine, no allergy tests were done; I am deadly allergic to it. When it entered me, first my whole body itched like ants were stinging me all over, even my eyes; then I felt as if I caught fire, my whole body! I then sneezed once, heard the doctor yell "having massive reaction" then my lungs just froze up and stopped, and then felt a big thump as my heart stopped, at this point I blacked out.

So I understand your heart stopped for five and a half minutes. That's a pretty long time... Do you remember anything while you were "gone"? When you "came back" how did you feel? Did you feel scared? At peace?
Did the time you were gone appear to be like the five minutes you were told you were gone or much more?

If you felt you were gone much longer, could you quantify how long it felt?
After I came to they told me I was clinically dead for five minutes and thirty seconds before they got my heart started again.

Now, this is hard to put in words.
I felt good, like a nice warm nap but like not a nap, it felt like a long time, weeks even, I was relaxed, happy; funny thing is I got the feeling I was not on my own, like I was being guided but don't remember seeing anyone.
I was just being taken care of; I now think I was being babysat till I could go back! Does that sound funny? I felt as if I was protected by non humans too, as if my past pets were there with me, hope this doesn't get too strange, I think cats have a type of being between both levels and wait for us, it felt like that.

But there was a something there (family etc.) that cared for me and brought me back to the crossing point; then I woke up, I felt sick from the treatment but felt good and relaxed. It is a funny thing but now I am no longer worried about dying anymore, my attitude is different, I know it's ok, I can't explain it and this is the first time I have even said anything about it.

Do you have any idea why it would feel longer than 5 minutes?
I have no idea why it felt like I was gone weeks, it JUST felt that way, like a nice long vacation/nap, but it did feel like weeks to me.

What did the doctors tell you after you came back? Was your condition the same or were you healed? If you were healed, did the doctors have a logical explanation for your recovery?
No more tests were done that day. They did transfer me to a different hospital for emergency open-heart surgery. As they were in the process of pushing me out to the theater the surgeon (told me later) stopped them and did an ultra sound on my heart.
He said, "something told him to do it". He couldn't see anything, so he did another endoscope down into my chest;
EVERYTHING was gone, another five minutes and my chest would have been cut open, two heart surgeons, two cardiologists, a hematologist said it was impossible for all the blood clots to vanish, called the heart association in Washington D.C. and they said they had never heard of it except once before, so who knows, maybe my friends on my nap did something but I also really believe that the positive power sent to me had a lot to do with it, we will never know for sure I guess.

All I know is one minute I am dying with a few hundred blood clots in me and I take a trip somewhere and next minute I am clear!

You told me that you remembered that I had said to you that "positive thinking" definitely helps the body and soul in the healing process. How did you apply your positive thinking on yourself?
I think that I kind of channeled the positive energy to me some how just by my need, it is beyond me so I am vague, but I did feel better, like I knew people were out there helping me.

Did you feel the energy of all the people sending you their healing thoughts?
I am not sure, this is all new to me, but something helped me come to terms with it all; that may have been part of it.

Do you feel mentally or spiritually any different now than you were before this incident?
Funny that, I feel mentally stronger because I don't fear death anymore, it now seems like it is going to be like walking through a door into a new room, a new beginning, a new world to explore, see all that I have lost and care for. What's to fear? I just have that feeling. Spiritually, no different in my belief, just happier about going, and I know I will be met and taken care of.

Would you like to add anything else?
I am still the same here, in your face, joker, short temper in traffic, worrier, workaholic, but can stop and feel the other side sometimes, and once in the quiet times I seem to see flashes out of the corner of my eye when relaxed as if something is running by, I think it is my cats watching over me as the Egyptians believed that their spirits are our protectors, who knows. Just could be old age, but I like to think I'm worth protecting! I hope all this rambling is a help, hard to put something like this in words. Bye for now."

What struck me in this interview is that it is not the common NDE with the separation from body, the lights, the floating. Gary's NDE is really interesting because this gentleman had an instant knowledge of being totally cared for, loved and protected while being in total darkness without feeling any fear at all, and without even questioning it.

Dr. Eben Alexander III, in his book "Proof of Heaven" talks about first getting in a dark place, where he felt at first comfortable as he knew nothing else.
He had no previous knowledge of his Earthly life, no preconceived idea of how it should be, since it felt totally normal to be there.
As he became gradually aware that this was not a place he would want to stay, he was brought up by and through a magnificent light to a place that defies description with words. Bliss is probably what he felt from that place which was vibrant in colors, sounds and life. But then he found himself in a totally pitch black place that he called "The Core", that emanated light from within. It was total darkness but the sensation of being totally loved and totally at peace and part of this darkness and light was again something that was hard to put into words when he came back.

It is fascinating to note the similarity between Gary's story of NDE which was at the most five and a half minute long (in Earth minutes) and the story of Dr. Eben Alexander III which could have potentially have been seven day long (in Earth days) as he was in a coma for seven days. But we don't know, because time has no meaning on the other side, clearly!

At one moment both were in total darkness but with absolutely no fear. And both felt an incredible amount of love and a sense of being taken care of.

In Dr. Alexander III's book he says he clearly received mentally three very powerful affirmations during his

NDE and those were:

"You are loved and cherished, dearly, forever"
"You have nothing to fear"
"There is nothing you can do wrong"

Both Gary and Dr. Alexander define their experience as life changing in the sense that they now both believe that our Consciousness is much more than what we commonly think and that there is absolutely nothing to fear, they are and will be taken care of.

But does it matter that Gary saw only darkness and Dr. Eben Alexander saw this incredible world with vibrant colors and sounds?

Absolutely not, because in the end our Consciousness creates the reality in which we feel the most comfortable! That is why, though there is a common thread or pattern of perceptions in NDEs, not one NDE will be identical to another one.

In the field of Consciousness studies, apart from the traditional medical study of the brain, I believe there are three directions where science will uncover clues to what Consciousness might be. The first one is NDEs. Because NDEs offer such a vast pool of data that can be accounted for and categorized, it is one clear path that should help scientist in their endeavor to unravel the mysteries of Consciousness.
The second possible evidential tools in Consciousness studies are Remote viewing and Controlled Remote Viewing and the third evidential tool is ADC (After

Death Communication) both of which subjects I will discuss in the next two chapters.

to binge ± binge / to not binge.

CHAPTER 24

Meeting Dr. Melvin Morse and Learning CRV (Controlled Remote Viewing)

If we look at the slit experiment again, where the electrons flow into a world of multiple possibilities, changing their properties from being a particle to a wave, it is very tempting to make the analogy with being psychic.

Given the opportunity of choice, the electron does not elect one choice, the electron creates a wave of possibilities and experiences both solutions, connects with both realities.
We humans, who carry the duality at our deep core level, have the ability to connect with multiple realities the same way, thanks to our right brain.
As soon as we try to rationalize and explain what's happening the electron loses the ability to experience the wave of possibilities.
We humans will lose our capability to connect with multiple realities as we grow up, being taught that everything has to be rationalized and explained.

Thank the Universe(s) we still have our dreams to save us!

What happens in the quantum world does not stay in the quantum world! It happens at our level too.

Controlled Remote Viewing or CRV is a method that has been designed and taught by Ingo Swann, the first psychic to come up with the idea that the information (sensory perceptions, dimensional perceptions and emotions) can not only be channeled but also systematically processed in order to retrieve very specific information.

It's a multi-level, multi-stage technique that allows the viewer to go deeper and deeper into the fabric of the informational Universe(s) using both one's right brain and left brain.

It was so revolutionary and the potential development so attractive that the US Federal Government decided to create a project called Stargate Project, which was active from 1970 to 1995, and was overseen and managed by the CIA and the DIA (Defense Intelligence Agency).

It had mainly a military purpose, one of spying on the Eastern Block and The Soviet Union, who were doing the same on their side!

But lately, CRV has been declassified and has become more mainstream though some of those who practice it still believe they are part of some sort of elitist group, which could not be further from the truth.

A few dissidents, like me, enjoy using CRV methodology mixing with their own "way" in order to give CRV other opportunities, other purposes.

Controlled Remote Viewing is a very systematic process with many stages.
You, the viewer, work with a monitor (or not). You are given a "target" (they are still using military terms) to which you are totally blind (meaning you know nothing of what you are supposed to remote view. You don't know what it is; you don't know where it is, etc.)

From a random generated number associated to the target, you start your Stage 1 CRV viewing by stating your name, where you are, the date and time you are starting the session and if you are with a monitor/partner, the name of your monitor.

As you start drawing lines on the paper, letting your right brain completely soak into the filed of information or what they call the "signal line" you get your first feel of movement and you are supposed to immediately state if you are dealing with a gestalt of land, or man made, or nature, or water etc. A gestalt is the essence or shape of an entity's complete form.

But now, on the contrary of pure mediumship where sensory perceptions come as they wish and are not "organized", CRV forces you to organize those perceptions.
If you are getting more information than the ones required in Stage 1, you basically have to ignore it, or acknowledge it on the side as AOL or AI (Analytical Overlay or Aesthetic Impact).

It forces your left brain to work at the same time than your right brain.

In stage 2, you can only "let in" sensory perceptions of colors and patterns and shape. You are not allowed to let in any emotional impact or big dimensional sensations, or even more precise perceptions such as abstract concepts or words.

Again, your left brain has to organize those perceptions.

In stage 3, you let in all dimensional sensory perceptions and start allowing "feelings " of the target and emotions that it triggers to hit you.

And it goes on like this with six main stages and many more, after that.

You also most of the time need a "monitor" to do the CRV with you. The role of the monitor is to keep in line of the signal, so that you do not go astray and lose yourself in unnecessary territory.

When your monitor feels like you have "hit the target" he or she will tell you and you have to either continue deeper or if it's just for the purpose of exercise, you start writing your summary report of your session. You might hit the target in a couple of stages or it might take longer. There are no rules about that.

To give you an idea of what it looks like, here is an example of CRV training I did just up to stage 3.

My monitor, located thousands of miles away, had selected a picture, "The target", for me to remote view.

The picture was kept secret and I did not have any knowledge of it.
I did not know what it was about, what it was representing or any details of it whatsoever.
As a matter of fact, I was only given a random target number.

I started the CRV. CRV sessions are done by hand.

So here are the transcript of my hand written sessions, that can be seen on the pictures in the next pages.

<u>Description of what we are supposed to do in Stage I (S1)</u>
• After being given a target random number
• Draw an ideogram (not a sketch) the pen has to run freely on the paper, it is how the site impacts your system subconsciously
• A – describe the movement of the pen in the ideogram and give 5 attributes
• B – Define the target or parts (gestalts) of the target (Natural/Biological/Structure/Land/Water/Manmade etc.)
(If several ideograms created, process with each ideogram the same)

<u>This is the transcript of what you see on picture 1</u>

• On the number 1) part of the ideogram, I wrote

A – Moving slowly in an undulatory motion – As for the attributes I wrote swaying, swishing, noisy background.

B – Natural (anything natural, trees, flowers, rocks etc.)
• On the number 2) part of the ideogram, I wrote
A – Going up at a small angle, going down nicely, peaking down and going back up immediately then moving in no particular shape and going down and around.

B – Biological (anything living) / Man made
The Cs that you see on the paper are the "correct" feedback given by the monitor when your perception is correct. When the perception is not correct, there is no feedback.

AOL means – Analytical OverLay – meaning your left brain is trying to explain too early what this is, you have to acknowledge it but put it on the side (hence written on the right side when it happens)

AI means – Aesthetic Impact – It is how the site, the target makes you feel

EI means – Emotional Impact – it is what the site shows as emotion or feels like

N means – Perception near right (almost right)
Site means – you have reached the site, "hit the target"
This is my stage I (S1) hand writing photo (Picture 1) as described in the previous page: (Monitor's name erased for privacy)

This is my Stage I (S1) handwriting photo (Picture 1):

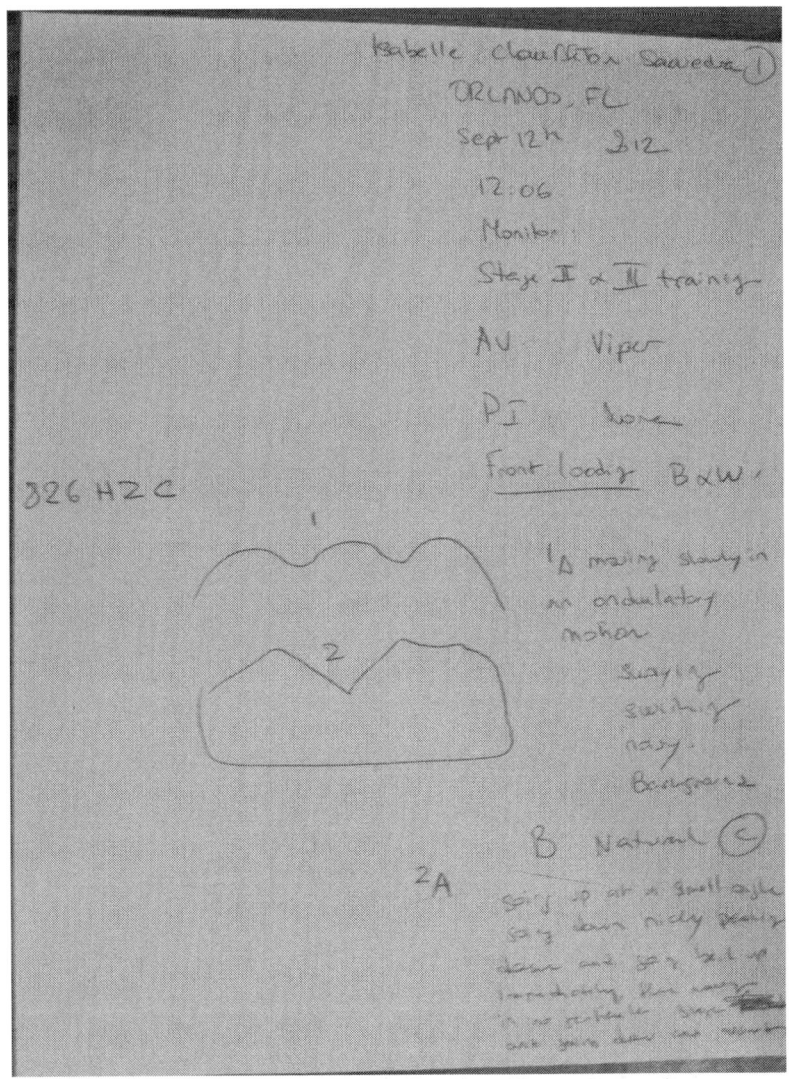

Picture 1 - *Photo Credit: Isabelle Chauffeton Saavedra*

Description of what you are supposed to do in Stage II (S2)

- This is the stage where you list all the perceptions you are feeling that pertain to your senses (colors, tastes, smells, sounds, touch, shapes etc.)
- You can also start to see very simple dimensionals (vertical, horizontals etc.)

This is the transcript of what you see on Picture 2

Clipity Clap sound
Gray
3 different levels (C)
Bustling
Different shades of gray (C)
But on the darker side
Not a layer, level
Large dark and light colors (C)
White component (C)
I can touch the white
Wind and movement (C)
Confusion – noisy
Square shapes
Round shapes

This is my Stage II (S2) handwriting photo (Picture 2):

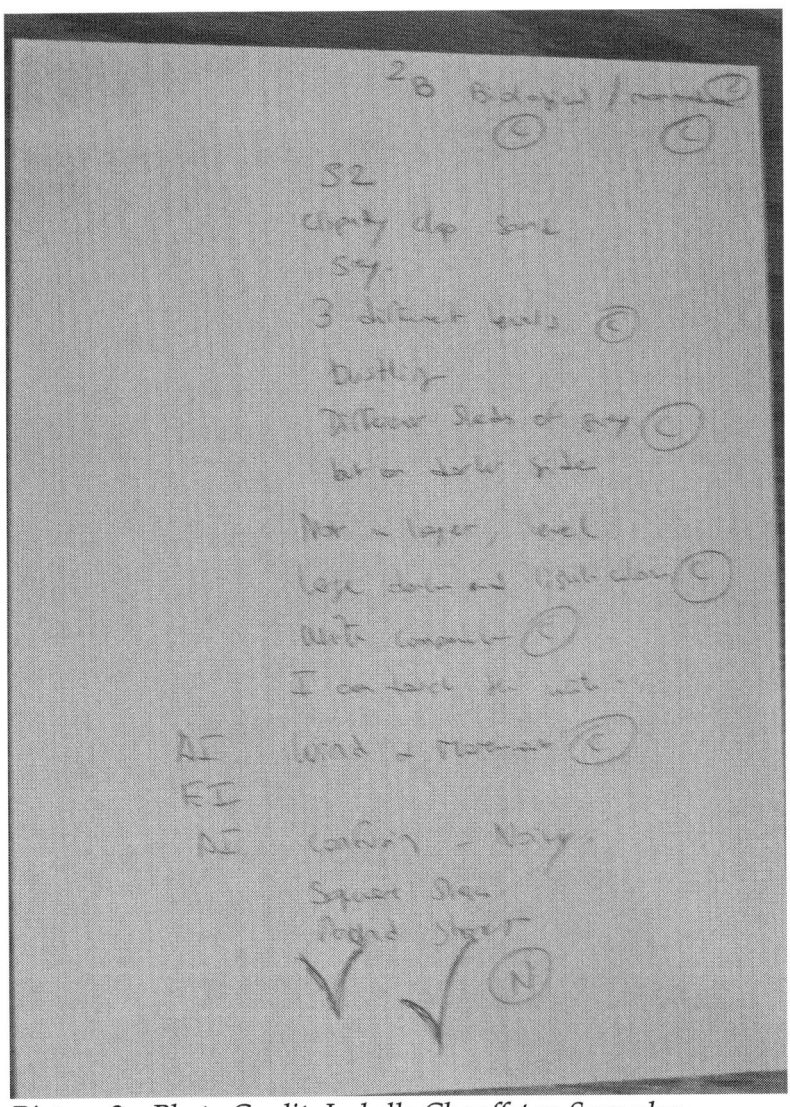

Picture 2 - Photo Credit: Isabelle Chauffeton Saavedra

Description of what you are supposed to do as you slowly move to Stage III (S3)

- This is the stage you start feeling more complex dimensionals
- You can start feeling the movement of the site if any
- And also let the site / target impress your feelings (AI) – and show you how it feels on site (EI)

This is the transcript of what you see on Picture 3

AI: Feels like want to rub my finger on it, stone would come out.

Move to wind and movement and noise
Circular movement (next to drawing)

Tornado   Site

End of Session

In this case, I hit the target at Stage III (S3) (Picture 3)

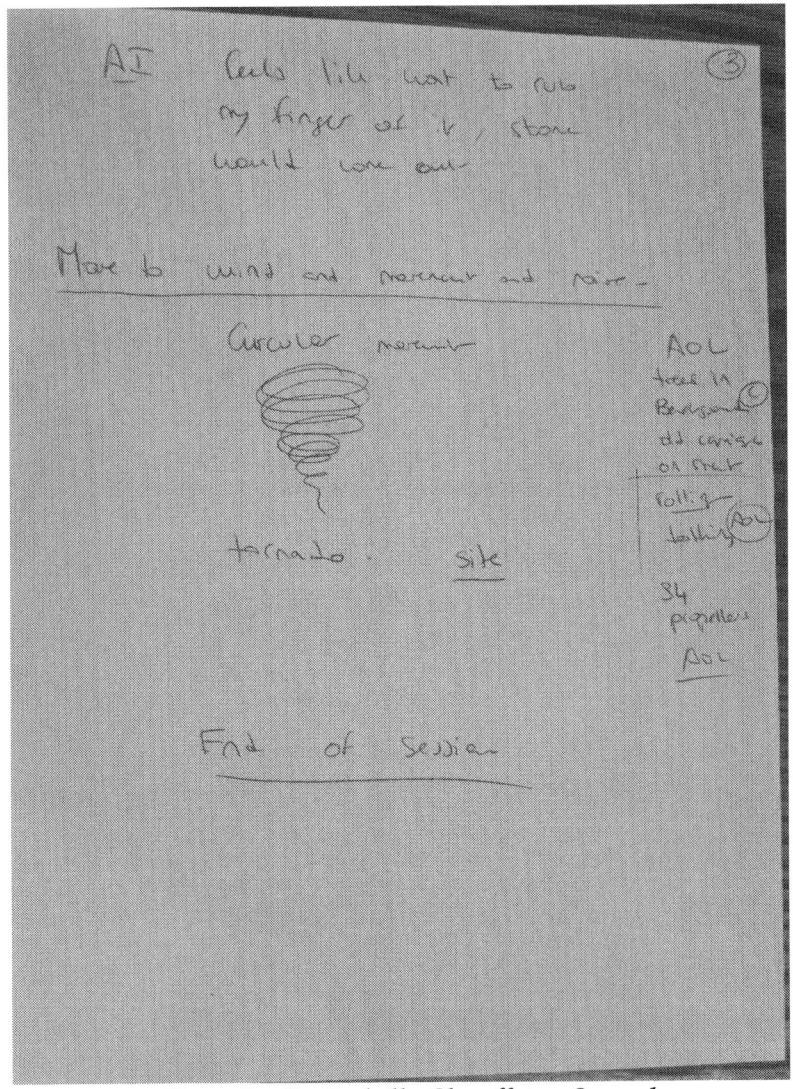

Picture 3 - Photo Credit: Isabelle Chauffeton Saavedra

(In a more complex site CRV, that would be the time when you start digging deeper to find intricate details about the site/target.)

Once the Site has been reached/contacted (meaning you found what is happening at the site, at the time the photo was taken), you end the session and write a session summary.

This is what I wrote: (Picture 4)

Session Summary
"The target presents aspects of natural with biological and manmade items. The Target site shows 3 different levels with different shades of gray but on the darker side. They are not layers; they are levels of large darker and lighter colors. There is a white component. There is a wind and movement aspect that goes with the target site and sort of a V shape. There are trees in the background. The target site made me feel like there is circular movement like a tornado.

End Session   12:26"

This is my session summary handwriting photo (Picture 4):

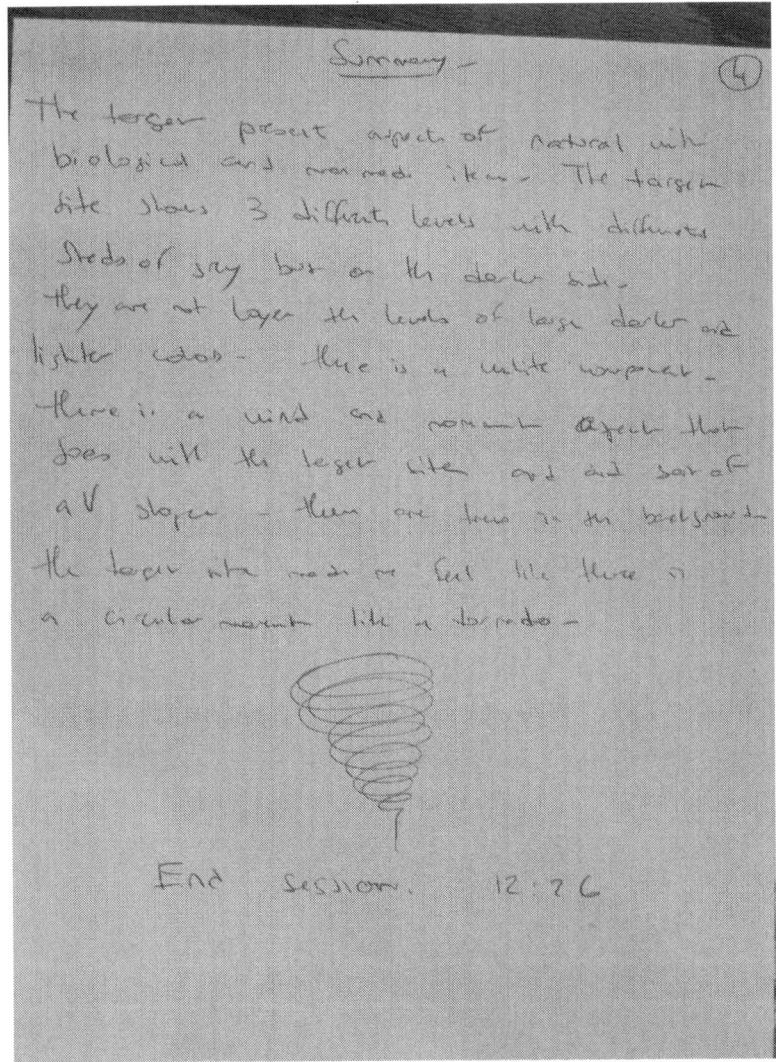

Picture 4 - Photo Credit: Isabelle Chauffeton Saavedra

Once the session is ended, the monitor can finally reveal the target she had kept secret. Note that this session was done at a distance. My monitor was thousands of miles away from me. We did our session using Skype.

The only thing I knew about the target picture she had selected was a random number she had given me at the beginning of the session.

This was the target site
(the photo kept secret from me the whole time):

Photo credit: Ruiz de Velasco / The Dallas morning news

Even if this example of CRV training seems pretty interesting, I find the methodology quite a bit restrictive in fact. CRV aficionados claim that it is the "only way" or the highway to get proper information from the informational Universe(s), but based on my experience I believe CRV to be only a tool of a much grander discipline altogether.
I find that combining CRV with pure mediumship for example allows achieving more precise connections.

In fact, what I have discovered working with both mediumship and CRV is that they are truly complimentary. CRV is a very good discipline that will focus on "things": places, natural settings, man made buildings, colors, shapes, dimensionals, everything related to left brain really. But as soon as it touches emotions, it is not as a great tool as it could be. You cannot restrict emotions; you cannot classify emotions. Emotions have to be set free otherwise they cannot flow properly.
That's when mediumship gets in the picture. In mediumship, emotions run high and they flow.

I find that mixing CRV and mediumship helps for example in the search of missing people. In the search of missing people you have to place someone who has disappeared (CRV) and retrieve information from that person about what's going on, where she is, how she is doing, who she is with or if she is in the light (mediumship). The use of both techniques enhances the process and gives more positive results.

In my quest and thirst of learning, I have had the pleasure and honor to meet Dr. Melvin Morse and we have become very close friends over the last few years.

Dr Melvin Morse is one of the founding fathers of NDE research.

First trained as an ER doctor, Dr. Morse started his medical career being a critical care flight physician, flying to remote places to help save people.
He saw his share of dying patients then, working hard trying to bring them back to life.

In 1982 Dr. Morse was called to work on a little girl who had drowned in a pool and was declared dead. Her heart had stopped for nineteen long minutes. Dr. Morse was able to bring her back and she recovered totally. But, upon her return, the little girl started to tell a tale of a journey she had taken while she was gone. It was the starting point for Dr. Morse into years of systematical studies and data accumulation on this phenomenon called Near Death Experience.

He also came to realize that a significant number of parents of children who died from SIDS had some sort of premonition or "feelings" something was going to happen and had recorded those feelings into journals prior to the death of their child happening, thus validating their visions.

His journey through the years led him to better understand our Consciousness and to conclude that it was something that was way beyond simple brain functions.

Lately Dr. Morse has been working on formatting new ways of using CRV for other purposes than what the government had originally trained their experimenters for.

When we met, through our Facebook pages, we started to talk about mediumship and CRV and how the two combined could achieve much more than what was actually being done in very closed circles.

Our first work together started with me being the object of his research.

I offered to become a guinea pig in experimental CRV at a distance.

The interesting part is, I am so used to getting in an altered state of Consciousness on a regular basis that during that particular séance which included many viewers all based in the state of Delaware (I was laying on my sofa in Orlando, FL) I instantly connected with the deceased uncle of one of the viewers who was remote viewing me!

It became clear then that we were going to work together.

Then, Dr. Morse included me as a non-official viewer for a scientific experiment led by a student of a University who was working on some specific molecule modification in a "secret study".

While my viewing was not featured in the final study, its content was used to illustrate how we can use mediumship viewing and CRV to help diagnose ailments to facilitate scientific studies by getting the researcher into the right direction, in a recorded presentation that Dr. Morse made during the 2012 IRVA annual convention.

Today I am working with Dr. Morse in developing a new CRV /mediumship protocol to further the research in the use of ESP as an added medical tool for diagnosis.

We want to use CRV to do good things, not to find "targets" that can be destroyed by bombs.

I believe that the accumulation of data under a controlled environment through the use of CRV and mediumship should be studied more systematically to show the direct connection between the power of detached Consciousness and nonlocal reality.

Science uses a very simple tool that is the formulation of a theory and then the repetitive experimentations to prove or disprove the theory.
Using NDE's data collection and studies, CRV and mediumship work in a totally controlled environment perfectly fits in the theory/experiment rules of science.

While I was given the pleasure of knowing Dr. Morse who had focused on NDE and Consciousness through the work of CRV, I had also the privilege of meeting one of the founders in the third possible evidential proposal for Consciousness not being a product of brain activity that is ADC (After Death Communication).

CHAPTER 25

Bill Guggenheim

Bill and Judy Guggenheim are the author of the best seller book "Hello from Heaven" which was the very first book to ever gather, categorize and bring to light a hand pick selection of 353 spontaneous experiences of ADC (After Death Communication) over more than 3000 stories collected originally.

Bill and Judy actually coined the term ADC (After Death Communication experiences) at the time they were collecting evidence.
They started their research in 1988, which placed them both, way ahead of their time. They gathered first hand stories of spontaneous ADCs over the fifty states and the ten Canadian provinces. It took them seven years to finish the study.

No one before had tried to regroup these experiences into a book that would clearly show a pattern and recurrent types of spontaneous after death communications.

I had the chance to meet Bill in the mid 2000's as he is living close to me.
After he responded to my no less spontaneous email about creating an after life and Consciousness convention we decided to meet during one of his book signing opportunities in a local book store.

I was very impressed by his approach to the whole concept of Consciousness and life after death.

The work that he and his former wife had done was tremendous.
Not only had they achieved a daunting job of collecting and categorizing the types of possible ADCs which came to a number of twelve, searching through thousands of accounts but they also had opened the door and cleared the way for a subject that had been considered taboo and non scientific, by placing ADC at the forefront for future research in the field of Consciousness.

In my early communications with disembodied energies, I had come across a lot of different ways they could make themselves known to me. But none of this was spontaneous; none of this was the will of those disembodied energies. I was forcing my way into their space and asking for a connection.

I understood from reading Bill's book that communicating with people who were no longer living in a body had to be a two way communication created by the openness of the space in between us.

I could not go in and "request" information. I would have to open my own Consciousness and expand it like I had done until now, but then I would have to let it be. And from that neutral field of possibilities, then the flow could happen.
(Like the Magellanic Clouds story, if you push too hard, you do not see…)

Once the flow would be established, the two-way conversation could happen, freely, from both sides.

I would have to place myself in the same state of mind as the people who experienced spontaneous communication, with no expectations whatsoever.

Reading Bill's book helped me refine my technique of mediumship and helped me understand that we exchange on a free will basis, not on command.

CHAPTER 26

Mastering my own reading technique
the importance of tangible validations in readings

Realizing the field of mediumship had been used and abused by all kinds of mean-spirited (pun intended) fraudulent people, it became obvious to me very fast that the work I was doing had to be taken with extreme caution and in an utmost ethical manner.

First of all the term medium in itself carries the stigma of years of abuse!

But I think to understand why the word medium is nevertheless both a bad and appropriate word and is worth keeping despite its challenging past interpretations, we need to go back to basics.

And yet again, to achieve that, we are going down the scientific path!

I refer to the Universe(s) as an information field and to Consciousness as a form of energy that we can tap into. An energy that might have a close relation to the electro-magnetic spectrum, since it seems that Consciousness can interfere with EMF meters and detectors.

As such, Consciousness most likely has a certain wavelength that we still have to figure out scientifically when it is not filtered through a brain.

But the interesting fact here is the definition of the word wave:

"A wave can be described as a disturbance that travels through a medium from one location to another location."
(http://www.physicsclassroom.com/class/waves/u10l1b.cfm)

We humans with bodies are just mediums in which Consciousness travels through!

As for psychic mediums, like me, we are no different. The only difference is that we have trained ourselves to be more attuned to the signal lines around us.

Not that we do have all the answers, but we work hard to recognize and channel the energies that are all around and within. We act like a radio fine-tuning in the different frequencies and wavelengths of Consciousness and we retrieve information.

Remember the double slit experiment in a previous chapter?

Being the medium for Consciousness reminds us that the wave state of matter was most likely the origin of everything, the memory bank of the Universe(s), including our "souls".
That is why Lavoisier, a French chemist and philosopher of the 18th century had a visionary idea when he said: "Nothing is wasted, nothing is created, everything changes to another form" We just pass from one state of existence to another without ever being lost. What works for basic chemistry seems to work for Consciousness as well!

How do we achieve this bridging? The key word that seems to work for every medium is "meditating", raising your awareness and practice, practice, practice!

We use our brain as a medium not only to process our own signal/wave of Consciousness but also the signal/wave of deceased or incapacitated loved ones' Consciousness (such as people in a coma or with Alzheimer's disease).

Then we play the signal through our body. That's why a medium is called clairvoyant, clairaudient and/or clairsentient, because it refers to what the body can feel and express while receiving and processing the signal/wave of a Consciousness.

***

In my years of practice I did not want to be labeled a Miss Cristal Ball that just does what she does for the fun of it or to extort money from grieving people in search of that one last connection with their loved ones.

So I started to work on a very clear "deal" with the disembodied energies I came in contact with. Once the neutral field of connection had been established and the two-way conversation could flow, I made myself clear that I would not take ANY MESSAGE until I was given tangible validations first.

In other words, in their precipitation and happiness to have found a way to communicate their love for their loved on this side, the disembodied energies were not allowed to say it, just yet...

I did convey and still do with every reading I do that with no validation from them showing their loved ones that the connection exists, there would be no message passed on!

It sounds a little harsh, but it is the only way, they can be sure their loved ones will have absolutely no doubt that they did receive a communication from the other side.

So no "I love you", No "I am with you every time you think of me" until you have disclosed who you are, and what you have done while you were in a body or provoking a spontaneous ADC that can be totally and undoubtedly recognized by your loved one.

Otherwise, they will always wonder.

The sitters will never doubt their deceased loved ones but will always do with the psychic medium and it is completely normal!

Tangible validations are the only way around that doubt.

Once there has been as many tangible validations as possible brought through the established connection between the deceased person and the psychic medium, then the messages and affirmations can come and be accepted as true.

Now I don't go in and get the validations, I don't ask questions. I just open the neutral field of communication and ask for "tangible validations" It's my only request. After that it's all free will of what they want to tell or not.

It is why sometimes it is difficult for some sitters because, they come with very specific expectations to a reading, such as "my crossed over loved one has to tell his name for me to be sure the connection is true"... Well.... It does not happen that way... If their loved one comes up with a validation such as: "three days ago you were wearing a purple shirt and went for a job interview", or " I died of a heart attack while canoeing on the lake"; that's pretty darn good validation to me! And if that is what he chooses versus his name to validate his presence, fine by me.

So it is very important during a reading to clearly explain how the process works. How MY process works, as each medium has his or her own process of course.

That too can be confusing for sitters.

What is very important to me is to make sure the sitter understands the only way to be able to truly recognize when a connection is happening is through facts and facts only!

Everything else is mumbo jumbo.

When all the facts that the disembodied energy has stated are laid out, then a more "loving" connection can occur.

The connection can go to a deeper level of Love and Light.

To create that safe environment of trust with a sitter is my priority.

Over the course of the years, the other particularity I developed in my technique, thanks in part to the practice of CRV is to recognize when my left brain is trying to over analyze an idea, or a concept that comes to mind while in meditation during a reading. Recognizing the intrusion and interference of left brain trying to rationalize a thought is the key to let go of the wrong information and not deliver it, or delivering it in its raw form.

A lot of time I am asked the same questions by fans on my Facebook page:
"How can I connect with my loved ones?"

The answer is always the same: "Practice, practice, practice". The more you do it the better you become at it and the more you are able to recognize deep in your soul when you have a true connection.

It is hard to explain in words, but the feeling that you are indeed on the signal line is very special. If you can't tell if you are on the signal line, you undoubtedly know you WERE on it when you snap out of it! The very action of snapping out of the signal makes you realize without the shadow of a doubt you had the connection.

Once you recognize this, you are able to determine each time you have a connection that you are indeed receiving the correct information.

Next comes the challenging task of minimal interpreting to preserve the authenticity and validity of the information.

In CRV, the method makes you itemize, rationalize and categorize every single perception you have pushing away other things that are not supposed to come up at a specific stage.
While I recognize the importance of pushing away certain impressions, the mere fact of categorizing and itemizing reduces the potential for more information to come. Pure CRV practitioners will tell you the opposite. They say that once you categorize all the sensory perceptions you receive, you make space for something else to come.

The point in connecting with the informational Universe(s) is to retrieve information and deliver it in the most non-invasive way to preserve the integrity of the information.

By opening to the field without trying to categorize, we let the flow be. When you are connected, it feels like going through a wormhole at the speed of light, things are coming fast and from all directions.

The real challenge is to not categorize but to actually let the information in no matter its shape or form and recognize which one is coming from the field of Consciousness and which one is coming from your ever wanting to interfere with the rationalizing left brain.

The brain is a very powerful tool that has been perfected by years of evolution to help the species to survive and thrive through every possible situation. Your left brain is always on the look out, trying to rationalize every single bit of information that comes in, because that's the only way to ensure the survival of the species.

Working with mediumship is teaching your left brain reverse-psychology and telling it that there is no danger, no reason for explaining or rationalizing, and thus it has to quiet down to let the other part of the brain acquire an infinite amount of new information that comes in with no purpose other than KNOWING.

Consciousness is all knowing. To filter consciousness through our brain is like trying to watch a high definition show on a black and white television! You will get the story, you will get the pitch, but you will be missing a lot of its quality and refined details.

One other thing I have implemented in the years of practicing mediumship is that I prefer to not be with my sitter. I prefer to be by myself. I also don't tell the sitter when I do the reading. Once the reading is confirmed, I will do it within a fourteen-day period. This way I establish an environment that is as close as possible as a double blind setting.

A scientific double blind setting experiment is an experiment during which neither party experimenting has the knowledge of what the experiment is about and how or when it happens to dismiss potential interference from one party or another in the experiment that could affect its outcome.

In the case of a reading, when the sitter and the reader are totally remote from each other, and when the reader proceeds in doing the reading without the sitter having knowledge about it, it dismisses any claim from skeptics for a cold reading.

After meditating, I sit at my computer and write all the perceptions that come to me chronologically. I do not edit any of it once I am done, except for spelling mistakes.
I then email the reading to my sitter who can only give me feedback once the reading is done and sent.

I also request absolutely zero information about the sitter or the person they wish to communicate with, I only want their relationship (mother, daughter, cousin, friend, etc.)

Actually if I have information it becomes more difficult for me as my left brain sees that as an opportunity to get in the way and tries to rationalize or explain... So no information is the key to the best reading possible!

You are probably thinking, all this is very technical but where is the spirituality in all this?

As you may have sensed already, I am not a religious person. I have the utmost respect for anyone's beliefs and religion as long as it does not interfere with human rights and freedom of one's body and mind.

Some of my sitters believe in a higher power or being and it's totally fine with me.

In fact no one knows really what created the Universe(s)... We can only speculate.
So all theories are equally correct.

The disagreement I have is with what us Humans did with these theories. In mathematics and physics, you put a theory out there and then you try to prove it or disprove it.
In most religions the theory becomes an axiom and that's where I diverge from it.
And based on this axiom, a minority of supposed chosen dictates the rules to the mass.

This is why as a medium, I chose the science path rather than the spiritual path.

Because I am not here to tell people that my way is the way. I am here to try to find how and why I believe our Consciousness is not linked to our brain activity and why because of that it might give us hope that we don't die and that we are indeed part of an ever evolving system that enables us to be linked to one another with no boundaries or frontiers.

There might not be a lot of spirituality in that but let me tell you, there is a lot of light (energy) and Love (our very human and animal way of being ONE all together).

And that's undeniable!

CHAPTER 27

Searching for missing people

Inevitably, as I was perfecting my art, I came across news on TV of people, snatched, disappearing for no apparent reasons, leaving behind them a trail of unanswered questions and families ripped apart by the anguish of not knowing where their loved ones are.

As a mother myself, nothing hurts my heart more than when a child has been abducted and there is no trace to follow. It is disturbing, enraging and I cannot stop the growing ache in my stomach that lingers long after hearing or reading the news.

In the cozy of my home I decided to start working on cases, by myself, cold cases, cases that had made headlines for months and went cold.

I never reached out to the parents or the families because it is a very personal journey to be on and I figured if my work were meant to be used, it would happen.

I did not want to intrude in their personal tragedy and add more anguish or give them false hope.

I figured, I have information and if the information comes true then my work just proves that I was on the right path, not that I could have saved the missing person or put law enforcement in the right direction; because it takes a team effort to use elements of a reading and analyze them to where it becomes useful information.
If the parents of cold cases came forward asking for help from me, then I would definitely work with them, with all my heart. It's a different synergy.

That's what happened, when Robert Demeck from the Way to Find organization approached me (names changed for privacy reasons). This group dedicates its mission to finding missing people around the world.

Robert created a group of fifteen anonymous viewers. People like me who are just happy to help.

When a request for a missing person comes to him from any where in the world, Robert creates a random generated number associated with the case and sends all fifteen viewers an email with that number for us to work on.

There are two ways of working. One is with what is called "front loading" and the other one is without "front loading".

What is front loading? Front loading is when you are given some information before you start your session about the case. Last place the person was seen, the name of the person, or even if it is a person; it could be a beloved pet that someone is trying to locate; or any pertinent information to the case.

Because of the way I work, always trying to tame my left brain from trying to rationalize everything, I prefer zero front-loading. Front loading for me is like chatter that becomes overpowering in my brain and hinders the true process.
Before hand information is a true obstacle for me.

No information is like having a clean canvas where you can let your soul paint the truth.

Looking for missing people is a serious endeavor. No one should ever take this lightly. It is not a fun game to play. At the end of the thought are a soul in distress and her family in disarray. It has to be taken with the utmost respect and the most profound gratitude, just to be involved.

While I am at the beginning of my endeavor in working with Missing People Research groups as I write this book, I can already tell you that my experience in both CRV and mediumship combined is a great tool.

It helps getting the information without letting the emotions pull you in a certain direction, but then again, once the information is down, the connection with the soul we are searching helps tremendously narrowing it down, as we are given to see, feel, smell and hear what our missing loved ones see, feel, smell and hear.

I use CRV to describe a position or place and then I place myself within that position and "become" them for a while using their vantage point.

Once every single viewer of the team has done his or her viewing remotely from where ever they live, Robert collects them all and assemble them into one single report where all names and private information about us have been erased and then it is sent to whom ever ordered the viewing, be it a family, law enforcement, a private investigator. We remote view people anywhere in the world.

The last person I was given to remote view was located in India, just to give you an idea. But before that it was a missing dog in Florida!

You never know what the next case will be and that is why it is interesting because, it's not about sensationalism, it's about truly working with your heart and soul to help people in distress.

CHAPTER 28

Finding an engagement ring in the laundry room!

On a lighter note, using Consciousness to do good things can also mean to help a friend in pre-matrimonial dire straight!

One day, I received this panicked message from a friend saying "You've got to help me! I can't find my engagement ring. I lost it. I thought I placed it on my night stand and now it's gone!"

So I said "sure let's see what I can do".

I started meditating and placed myself in her home (which I had never been too, they had just moved in).

And the funny thing is that I was sensing the ring travelling from one place to another. First I saw it dropped close to their bedroom window, but then I immediately felt that it had been picked up again and moved.

I went through every room in the house in my mind and each time, I was coming back to the laundry room.

The perception was stronger and stronger…

I told her I felt her cats were the culprits and they had actually played and brought the ring in the laundry room.

She then told me that her cats, loved to sit in the laundry basket when it was full of laundry…

So I told her "Don't look further, look exactly there!" And voila! The ring appeared in between piles of laundry!

It was such a relief as her wedding was coming pretty soon and the poor thing was in complete panic mode!

Using mediumship to do good, that's what every single medium should set herself or himself to do, no matter what it is for, as long as it brings comfort to the person you are doing a séance for, it should be the only goal.

CHAPTER 29

Describing a house to a T while trying to retrieve information on a robbery.

This chapter is about showing how the perceptions come to my mind.

In this particular reading, I used a mix of CRV technique and my own mediumship process. What you are a bout to read is the transcript of a reading done at a distance, as usual after I was sent a request to find information on a robbery that had happened in a house thousands of miles away from where I live.

A nice lady whom I have never met in person became a fast friend over Facebook when we connected through our dogs. She and I own two sister dogs from the same litter/breeder and we all love our puppies! But that's about it of what I knew of my Facebook friend's life at the time of the reading I did for her!
One day, my friend sent me a picture of an earring, just asking me if I could feel anything about it, without any other mention of anything else.
The earring picture she sent me is actually the one earring left from a pair. The other earring along with other things had been stolen a few weeks before when

my Facebook friend got robbed during the night at her house. At the time of the reading, I did not have this information; I was just asked to see what I felt about that earring.

Here is the transcript of my reading with my friend's remarks and explanations (notes in italic and photos sent by my friend to me post reading to validate my perceptions)

I never saw pictures of her house until the day I received her validations post reading and did not know about the earring being robbed until that day either.

"Carnivals
Fairground *(My grand daughter was just on a fairground showing chickens that she raises just for the shows)*
2nd earring fell twice *(Did the thieves drop the earring twice while leaving? they clearly dropped this one at least once!)*
Once in between breasts LOL
Partridge? *("On the first day of Christmas, my true love sent to me a partridge in a pear tree." The pair of earrings was given to me on Christmas day by my true love.)*
Turning, and dancing around and slowly waltzing
Someone has the 2nd earring
Kiosk or Merry go round type of structure
Purple
Brown
Green

229

This is a merry go round purple (top draperies alternate white and purple colors, horse poles are purple) and brown (wood structure) with green jewelry on the horses that is sitting in my Living room.

Photo credit: Shelly Aberton

Straight, round, noisy *(A circle but straight. This is what the thieves stood on to get into my house.)*

Photo credit: Shelly Aberton

Smiling lady with glasses *(might be linked to the thieves?)*

This earring was found *(it was found on the floor after I realized I had been robbed)*
It's waiting to be reunited

Cotton candy smell
Clap sound
Horseshoe sound *(all linked to the Merry go round impression?)*
Bustling come and go, come and go *(I believe this is what the thieves were doing)*
Turning

Prize ribbon. Trees around and open field too. There is a house in the background, white, with sort of an old plantation, old farm feel. Someone's getting married or there is a celebration of some sort.

This is a painting I have in my living room that can be described by your vision above

Photo credit: Shelly Aberton

There is some hay in one corner behind the structure or the kiosk or merry go round
The kiosk is to my left, the house in the far is to my right like at 3 o'clock and then at noon it goes a bit up hill. The hay is at 11:00 o clock.
The bustling goes away and there is sadness coming in
Loneliness
It's over
It's gone
The kiosk has drapes all around.
(This describes the scene after the thieves left and I woke up all alone in my house realizing I had been robbed, I felt loneliness, realized "it was gone", and great sadness came over me)

The person who is linked to this earring saw this, she was there, it is very familiar to her. There is a sense of I belonged there.
(I was robbed in my sleep in my house)

This earring has been moved from its original location.
(Robbed and dropped by the thieves, the other one has been taken)

I now have a young lady appearing to be from the 50s in my mind's eye, with a typical Audrey Hepburn high bun and a 1950 dress.
She's claiming the earring.
Many people have commented that my daughter Trisha looks like Audrey Hepburn. She dresses very elegantly. She loves pearl jewelry.
{…}

It took 2 to take off your cast. I don't know what it means but she's telling me to say, "It took 2 to take off your cast"....
(The cast I had on when the robbery happened was my 2nd cast. The day before I tried to have my doctor give me a new one but he said no because I didn't have a valid reason. The intruder left one of my gates open and Mayzie took off. I walked thru wet grass and mud to see if I could see her. My cast was gross. When I went to the doctor, I told him about the robbery, I convinced him to put on a new one. That was not part of his plan)

The energies are fading away.

In this interesting first reading about my friend's earring, I just validated the fact that there had been an intrusion based on the sensory perceptions...
The fact that the connection took me to the very house where the robbery happened and lead me to see from within was a clear indication that I was on the right path, on the "signal line".

The rest of the story cannot be revealed by respect for privacy... but a few clues coming from this reading led to believe that the source of the robbery could be found. But it shows how we can use CRV and mediumship to get very clear details about situations and locations without the shadow of a doubt.

CHAPTER 30

The importance of cross validations in mediumship
"The Glorying, a spirit rescue"

As we are talking about tangible validations and remarkable details coming out of readings and séances to solve all kinds of issues or just connect with loved ones, it is important to notice that when we get cross validations by different people at the same time about the same "signal line", it becomes the most powerful tool of evidential process.

A timely non coincidental sequence of events between August Goforth author of The Risen located in Manhattan, NY, Rob Smith EVP specialist and researcher located in Australia and myself in Florida, lead to an "energy" rescue and acknowledgment of a young man who left his body suddenly and found himself as pure Consciousness at the very young age of fifteen, lost for just a little while before being rescued by a loving great aunt who had passed away way before he did...

I have asked permission from August, to use the transcript of his blog about this incredible sequence of events that just shows how the connection we made were so valid, so important and so comforting.

It is important for me to remind that neither Rob Smith nor I had any previous knowledge of this young boy's existence or passing, or any close relationship with August to the point that we would know him and details on his family. We knew nothing other than August's young nephew had just passed away.

Here is the story as August told it on his blog on July 23rd 2013

"The challenging heat wave we've been enduring here in NYC has finally abated after a warm and wonderful rainfall late last night - so now I can live with the windows open, instead of freeze-drying myself in an air-conditioned environment. Granted, it's 84 F with 69% humidity, but it's so much better than 105/85!

It was especially magical running into a special friend and neighbor, Noveh, also on her way home from work, and we stood and chatted with our arms wide open to embrace the delicious drops as they fell, chatting excitedly about our upcoming visit to Lily Dale in mid-August.

Spirit found us the perfect person to take care of our crowd of cats while we're gone. Incidentally, "crowd" is not correct ... the terms for describing a bunch o' cats is clowder, clutter, pounce, clout, nuisance, glorying, or glare. Take your pick. In my case, either a nuisance or a glorying would suffice.

Some of my closer friends know about the tragic event that launched the transition of my nephew, Ty (Tristan).

After only 15 years on this planet, he managed to leave early last month, much sooner than any of us expected -- although his father later confessed he wasn't surprised, as Ty was far too brilliant and intense for the Earth, burning his candle at all ends at all times.

He had been engaging in target practice with his pellet guns, at his best friend's house. Both he and his friend were shooting tin cans and bottles in the back yard. When they finished, they ran over to the picnic table, Ty tossing his gun carelessly on it. Unknown to him, the gun was still cocked, and when it hit the table, discharged a small metal pellet into the area just below Ty's sternum. He must have felt something odd, for he remarked to his friend, "I know this is weird, but I think I've been shot." And then, within a few seconds, his face turned blue, his body white, and he fell over in a faint. At that point, he was ejected from his body, which was shortly on its way to the hospital in an ambulance; the body expired by the time it got there.

My brother got the news while at work, and called my sisters, who rushed to the hospital. They in turn called my other brother, who then texted me with the news - all of which happened within 15 minutes from the moment Ty had been shot. I had been chatting with spirit rescuer and EVP expert, Rob Smith and the medium, Isabelle Chauffeton Saavedra on Facebook at the time - which now seems was not a coincidence, or even a synchronicity, but a Spirit Orchestration - so I was sharing everything with them as it was happening from my smart phone as I stood in the kitchen.

Rob said he would set up his EVP equipment and start broadcasting in Ty's direction.

Needless to say, I was going into the shock one experiences at times like this, and also into trance. I could feel Ty as if he were standing right next to me, as well as his own shock, fear and confusion.

Then I could see that he was looking down on his body, and unable to comprehend that it was him. He thought he was still embodied, and was becoming rapidly panicked when his friend, who was crying and screaming, paid no attention to him.

I then heard the voice of my Aunt Agnes, who was the first family member to transition, many years ago, and a very special favorite of mine, say to me, "I'm here with some other family members, sent to meet and escort him to his new Home ... but he's not responding to us ... apparently he can't or won't see and hear me even though I'm right next to him! He's never met me and doesn't even know who I am, so there's a frustrating gap here -- we need you to help us, now - call to him and get his attention!"

Immediately I began speaking to Ty in a loud but calm and authoritative voice: "Ty, this is your Uncle August, I'm here to help, listen to me!"

I was right to rely on his exceptional intelligence and insatiable curiosity, as he got still and listened as I quickly and succinctly explained what was happening and what had to happen next.
"Stay still and don't move - our Aunt Agnes is coming to help you right now," and I flashed a mental picture of her to him. And then, our Aunt announced, "We've got him, thank you! Let's go!"

I also heard many others in Spirit exclaiming and chattering away in happy and congratulatory voices: "Welcome!" "Oh, you're going to love it there!" "It will be so much more fun than you can imagine!" and so on. Definitely a glorying, clowdering clutter!

Less than 15 minutes had passed. I was exhausted and weeping from the sheer intensity of it, and then realized that I was also incredibly hungry.

This was very annoying to me ... now? I can't even think of eating! But my blood sugar had plummeted so low, I knew I had to do something.

I picked up one of the takeaway menus on the kitchen counter. I could definitely eat pizza, should I order it? I mused to myself. But it's so hot today; I can't eat pizza on such a hot day.

*At that moment, Rob texted me via Messenger, "I just got the words, '**hot pizza**' over the equipment, sounds like an older lady's voice. Does that make sense?"*

As I was answering him, Isabelle messaged, "I'm picking up that your nephew is now with an older woman, possibly a great aunt?"

What validation! The three of us were ecstatic!

Since then, I've been checking in on Ty, and he's having the time of his life. Finally, he says, he feels truly free, and he can do so much more with his mind now.

He doesn't miss the confinement and restrictions placed upon having a material earth body. But he continues to grieve for his father's terrible loss, and to be frustrated at not being able to help him.

Although he's receiving a lot of education on how to provide comfort to those he left behind, and I can see that it's slowly but surely helping my brother revive.
 Many have asked me why I don't share this story with my brother, but there is a Risen way of doing things, which always and firstly requires that the person in need must, in some way, ask for help.
Help cannot be forced in any way. If and when he asks, of course I will hopefully recognize that moment and take the plunge - he knows nothing about my mediumship, and is a professed agnostic on an atheistic fence.
I therefore must rely on my complete trust in the Risen's mysterious ways of orchestration, and stay out of the way to let this particular tapestry unfold, as it must and will.

By the way - I ordered a glorying of pizzas."

What happened there was an incredible sequence of events that brought cross validations in mediumship to its highest evidential level.

I am always searching to achieve the best tangible validations, again, always to make sure we have a true connection, to show that we are indeed on the signal line of the energies we are trying to connect with.

When a sensitive and brilliant author like August, an Electronic Voice Phenomena specialist like Rob and a medium like me get the same information at the same time being so totally distant from one another, it is a phenomenal achievement in the work of Consciousness.

Not only it proves that we were all connected to the signal line of August's nephew and aunt (great aunt for the young man) but that each type of connection that was made, whether through mediumship or technical equipment was valid individually and collectively.

It also clearly shows that distance is not a factor, bringing us back to the Bell theorem and its non-local reality theory.

Imagine if these non-scheduled types of events could be replicated in a true controlled scientific environment! The impact would tremendous!

> This is exactly what I am working towards and vouching for in my daily endeavor!

CHAPTER 31

Deathbed visions

Grab the signal line and listen! That's exactly what our loved ones do when they are ready to release their energy back to the Universe(s).

Many a report has described terminal patients or elderly people in hospice care talking to invisible entities, getting all smiles and happy, raising their own hands towards invisible hands, having full conversations, singing.

Deathbed visions were studied and recorded as early as in the 1920s. Dr William Barlett, professor of Physics at the Royal College in Dublin came across a story his wife, a doctor had told him about a woman that had just died after giving birth.

The woman right before dying had sat on her bed saying she was seeing her deceased father in a beautiful place and her sister as well. The interesting part of the story is that the woman did not know her sister had passed a few weeks before. It had been kept hidden from her to preserve her health.

Professor Barlett was so fascinated by the story that he decided to create the first systematic study about deathbed visions and eventually collected the results in a book called by the same name that was published in 1926.

Years later other studies confirmed what Professor Barlett had found:
Most of the people experiencing deathbed visions say that dead relatives are coming to take them away. Their visions usually last a few minutes and are very vivid. They are happy to see their relatives. All patients regardless of the upbringing, the beliefs or the religions are experiencing deathbed visions without any distinction. Drugs are not a factor.
People having deathbed visions appear to be actually extremely lucid when experiencing them.

Deathbed visions are essentially an amazing change that happens in the state of our Consciousness. Because our body is getting ready to shut down, because our brain is not trying to rationalize every single piece of information it is bombarded with, it is actually freeing our Consciousness from its restraint.

Imagine living your whole life in a fog and all of the sudden, a hole appears in the dense mist and while you are immediately attracted to the opening, you discover that there is a whole "new" world beyond it, because you can hear the cheers and you can see other people, people you love peeping through the hole.
Wouldn't you be ecstatic?

Unfortunately, despite the few studies that have been conducted, deathbed visions are still often disregarded by the medical community and many a time considered as "hallucinations part of the dying process".
The worst part is that they are often "treated" with heavy sedative medication to "calm the patient".
My first reaction is why do you want to "treat" something that is not broken?
And my second one is, even if you think the patient is having hallucinations, which we know it is not the case, why would you want to take away from a dying person the joy of seeing and meeting with their dead relatives? Just to make you feel better as a doctor, for having prescribed the right medication for the right mental ailment? To a dying person? Really?

Deathbed visions are a very sensitive matter to me because it goes to show that there is a huge lack of compassion in the medical system.

Nowadays doctors don't have the "time" to acknowledge their patients feelings. So to make them feel better, when there is no need to make them feel better, they prescribe drugs, because that's what a doctor does.

If it were not for the work of devoted volunteer hospice workers such as Amy Cavanaugh, patients with deathbed visions would never have the chance to fully experience their beautiful encounters.

I met Amy through Facebook. Amy is always commenting with down to Earth no nonsense wit on others' posts in forums and groups related to life after death, meditation, mediumship and the like. She is a fan of my page and we quickly became friends because I liked her direct style of saying the things that need to be said.

As I got to know her, first virtually I realized Amy has a passion for helping people. She is a diamond in the rough. Her heart is big enough for all the many people she meets and heals with her presence.

Her calling: visiting dying people in hospice and just be with them.
Just holding a hand, listening to their story, singing with them, laughing with them, being silent with them. She is the last connection with the physical world for many dying patients who can count on her loving presence to accompany them through the hole in the fog, into the light.

Meeting her physically was no different. When we met for the first time, it was all about singing and her warm personality lit the room wherever she would stand.

When she let me know that Dr Eben Alexander III, author of Proof of Heaven was going to be giving a lecture close to our town, we decided to make it an outing and invited our friend Dr. Melvin Morse to come with us to share a beautiful day filled with love and light.

Amy is the type of person you would want your loved one to hold her hand if you were not able to be there for them at this crucial moment of expanded

Consciousness when the body dies.
She is strong and funny but with the heart as big as a whale's or a mermaid... should I say...
Amy has a passion for mermaids. Don't mermaids bridge two worlds like Amy does with her work as a hospice volunteer?

In Amy's own words....

"Like everybody, I both feared and avoided death.

Other people's deaths were always about me-me being sad, me being scared, what I was losing. Then in 2010, I had the privileged of helping my husband die.

Interestingly, we were separated when I learned he had leukemia. He had a wide range of medical issues and was heavily over-medicated. The side effects of the medication made him impossible to live with, he was verbally abusive, erratic and unreasonable.

However, when I found out he was ill, I knew I needed to be there for him. I learned that we die as we live and Keith's death was just as chaotic and erratic as he was. Sharing that time with him was the greatest blessing I ever received. His final illness lasted about 10 months.

During that time he was in and out of several hospitals and became severely addicted to pain pills, which in the end took his life.
He actually died when I was in the bathroom, but in the hours before his death, I had the sensation of traveling into the light where I met of all people, Jesus.

While I was certainly lost and confused after he died, right from the start I sensed his ongoing presence and that our connection was far from over. In the 2 years since he died my life has been enriched in ways that are almost impossible to describe. For one, Keith carried me through the final illness of my brother and helped him transition to spirit.

My brother was also a complicated guy who died a complicated death. I also became a Hospice volunteer and was asked to host a radio show where I speak freely about death and dying with candor, humor and wonder. My hospice patients and their families vary.

Many are very religious, others are very spiritual and some just put their head in the sand. What I have learned is that dying is a highly personal experience and the only thing we can do is be present for that person and be willing to share their space.

Sadly, I find that Hospice is still primarily focused on the physical aspects of death and dying and while they have spiritual counseling and chaplains on staff, it is mostly about the body. The reactions of the family members to the deathbed visions of the dying vary.

Some are upset by them because they feel that their loved ones are losing their minds. Others try to rationalize them in terms of some sort side effect.
I will say that those who accept them for what I know them to be, find great comfort and stay connected with their loved one through the dying process as if they systematically hand over the caregiving to their loved ones in spirit.

It is my dream that we continue to have open and honest conversations about the process of death and dying and speak with our relatives about what it will be like when some of us are living and others are in spirit.

We have largely institutionalized death, just as we have so many other aspects of our lives. I believe that the only way that we can personalize death is to speak about death, speak about what we believe happens when we die and speak about what we would like to happen.

I still believe that the loss of life is very sad and I do not think that should be overlooked or downplayed but I think that it is important that we not become overwhelmed with sadness during the dying process. I like to equate a dying person to a bride. During the dying process, they are the center of attention and we should do what we can to keep the focus on the dying person. We should talk to them, not about them and we should embrace and even ask the dying about deathbed visions and their dying experience. Not only does this keep us in communion with the dying, but it is also a profound learning experience.

I talk to people about death and dying as often as possible and have created a clearinghouse of information through my organization-The Coiste Bodhar which is the Irish word for death coach. While the word refers to a vehicle as opposed to a person, I like the concept of coaching people in preparation of this very important milestone."

CHAPTER 32

Demystifying the whole "Ghost hunting" business
We need to find new terminology for Consciousness and the whole area of research on Consciousness.

From the young girl wanting to experiment table tipping with her dad to reaching out to disembodied Consciousness today, my journey has been quite a roller coaster. And I don't even like roller coasters!

They scare me and make me nauseated. But my life has been the best roller coaster I have been given to experiment.

Every single choice I have made was clearly orchestrated in a way I could not understand when I was making those choices, but each choice makes complete sense looking back on them today.

Seeing my grand father the night he died, above his music stand, sensing the despair from the man who jumped to his death in Paris, connecting with Dustin who was a prisoner of his own body, all these events were defining moments in my life that created a new spark, a new opening in the veil and raised more questions, tickling my thirst of knowledge.

Because of my non-invasive approach when I connect with Consciousness, I never dare ask them the where and how. Somehow I feel it is not my position to ask. I feel I would not be able to understand the answers even if they were given to me.

It's ok to bridge between matter and energy but don't ask how all this is working.

Even if I don't ask the disembodied energies, I still want to figure it out; that is why the world of Science is such a perfect tool.

I experiment and see if this could match any scientific hypothesis already made… And if they are not made yet, well, why can't I make one?
And in the process, I reunite people! How wonderful is that!

Today, the media seem to have been totally engulfed in the "paranormal".
Oh, how I dislike this word!

There is nothing that annoys me more than when people talk about the "paranormal". Something paranormal is something that is beyond explanation by science.

But really, why would seeing apparitions, hearing voices, recording them, capturing movement with technical equipment, be not normal?

It has happened since the beginning of time, it's part of how our world and Universe(s) work! **Everything is normal. Because everything was created the way it is.**

Take for example a simple explanation for being us, with a body or seeing an apparition.

Science has a theory that is about to be proven by CERN (the accelerator of particles in Switzerland) that the Universe(s) is just made of tiny specks of energy and that there is a field all over the Universe(s) called the Higgs field (named after the physicist who came up with the theory).

This theory says that energy by itself could not agglomerate to create matter as we know it (protons, neutrons, electrons that form the atoms).

But when those tiny specks of energy travel through the Higgs field, they gather mass a bit like a spoon that you dip into honey, the honey slows down the spoon and agglomerates around it to the point you can lift the spoon and the honey sticks to it.

All of us and any conscious being in the Universe(s) has at one point or another been a spoon traveling through honey, gathering mass to become a body.

If energy has to hit the Higgs field to acquire mass and turn into matter, I'd say it would be pretty easy to extrapolate that when we die, some how we are "ejected" from the Higgs field... We are still here, just not manifesting anymore... It would also explain mists, partial or full body apparitions... for one moment we would find our way back into the Higgs field and able to materialize but I guess our level of energy would not be enough to sustain the state of matter and we would disappear again, and become a clean spoon traveling in the vastness of the Universe(s) waiting to cross another field of honey or not...

There is nothing not normal in the manifestation of energy! We are made of energy at our deepest core level. The Universe(s) is energy.

When we stop sensationalizing after death communication and studies on Consciousness and we keep any and all religions out of the picture, we will finally have a "normal" subject that can be treated with the same respect than quantum physics or theoretical physics.

We need to rethink the terminology in our field and find new terms for psychic mediums, paranormal, ghosts, hauntings, possessions and the like.

There is no such thing as a ghost! There is a person whose Consciousness once filtered by a body and brain has been released to the fabric of the Universe(s) to continue its expansion and balance its entropy. That Consciousness is so beautiful and unique and vast that there is no definition that would fit its beauty in our vocabulary, but we can certainly come up with a much better term than ghost!

These terms are the laughing act of a field of research that is dragged down by their negative aspects.

Yes I go to homes and public places that have presented "unexplained" phenomena and try to capture evidence with technical equipment; yes I do readings; yes I experiment on Consciousness by practicing CRV and mediumship and work on finding missing people; but NO I do not work in the paranormal field!

I am just one tiny spec of light in the Universe(s) trying to understand how all this works and if my work brings comfort and closure to just ONE person, helping this person to realize he or she is more than just a body with a mind but a beautiful Consciousness temporarily living la vida loca on Earth, then my job is done.

CHAPTER 33

(God) Consciousness is the answer we all have been waiting for

Michael Faraday who was a famous chemist and physicist received very little formal education and knew little of higher mathematics, such as calculus; and yet he went on to became one of the most influential scientists in history. He is referred, by some historians, as the best experimentalist in the history of science.

I would not dare comparing myself to Faraday but I am just taking his example to show that no one needs a PhD or a MA behind one's name to postulate valid hypotheses.

I know from experimenting that Consciousness goes far beyond the chemical and electrical processes of our brains. And I will strive for the rest of my life at being the best experimentalist I can be to prove it.

I believe that Consciousness should be the most researched field of science because Consciousness is the key that will unlock all the answers to our humanity, our presence on this planet and the reasons for our very own existence within the Universe(s)

We are stardust, but the stars bear our Consciousness. And if we were told as children how beautiful and expandable our Consciousness is, instead of reducing it to what we see through our eyes and hear through our ears, and feel with our hands, maybe, maybe we would be living in a better world; where love, compassion and empathy would be the three main driving forces of our humanity on Earth.

Every day, when I drop my children at school, my six year old daughter always tells me before we part for the day: " Mommy, don't forget to send me hugs, kisses and waves; I will feel them and I will do the same to you". And I do feel the "waves" she sends me. It is simple, but it's a step towards teaching our children to use their Consciousness to their fullest potential.

It is by encouraging the next generations to open to receive and send through their "God Consciousness" that we will help them expand their capability for Compassion, Empathy and Love and create a better world to live in.

About the Author

Isabelle Chauffeton Saavedra was born in France just one year before the first man put foot on the moon. Raised in a loving family, she quickly realized that neither her sensitive mother, who believed in a "traditional God" and practiced his teaching everyday helping people, nor her scientific father who had to have proof of everything to believe, had the answers to her questions about life and death.

From a very young age after being shielded from the death of her maternal grandfather, she started to show a keen interest in the matter of life after death.

Driven by many personal spontaneous psychic experiences, she engaged her life in many different paths, but always staying the course: Finding answers about Consciousness and its very own existence beyond bodily incarnation.

After studying mathematics and physics as a freshman in college in France, she took a different route that led her to travel to three different continents to finally settle in the USA.

After being successful in the corporate world for about twenty years she gradually realized her real calling had been within her since the very beginning.

Once she created a family, it became obvious she had reached the point of no return and had to let her passion lead the way to a new chapter of her life: Being an experimentalist psychic medium, with a scientific twist!

Today, Isabelle enjoys reconnecting people from different levels of Consciousness while tackling the most important questions about our presence in the Universe.

Setting herself apart from an often time sensationalized media driven industry, Isabelle Chauffeton Saavedra strives to promote an ethical and respectable form of psychic experimentalism.

Her deep interest in understanding how consciousness and quantum physics, two subjects that seem diametrically opposed, can be so very much closely intertwined takes her readers through logical yet emotional new ways of seeing how we are all connected.

She keeps a Facebook page under her name and can be found on her website for informational blogging and private readings.

www.survivalofconsciousness.com
Or email at **isabelle@survivalofconsciousness.com**

Photo of Isabelle by Jennifer Helton Photography